THEORY OF A
MULTIPOLAR WORLD

ALEXANDER DUGIN

THE
THEORY
OF A
MULTIPOLAR
WORLD

ARKTOS
LONDON 2021

ISBN	978-1-914208-16-4 (Paperback)
	978-1-914208-17-1 (Hardback)
	978-1-914208-18-8 (Ebook)

TRANSLATION   Michael Millerman

EDITING   Constantin von Hoffmeister

COVER & LAYOUT   Tor Westman

🌐 Arktos.com   f fb.com/Arktos   ◉ 🐦 ✈ @arktosmedia

Contents

1

Introduction

Multipolarity: Definition of the Concept and Delineation of Meanings

The First Efforts toward an Elaboration of a TMW

FROM A PURELY scientific point of a view, a full-fledged and complete Theory of a Multipolar World (TMW) does not exist today. We will not find it among the classic theories and paradigms of International Relations (IR).[1] We will also search the newest postpositivist theories in vain. It is not fully elaborated even in the most flexible and synthetic domain — in the sphere of geopolitical studies, where much is often comprehended that in IR remains outside the frame or is interpreted too unfairly.

Nevertheless, more and more works devoted to foreign policy, global politics, geopolitics, and international relations proper are dedicated to the topic of multipolarity. A growing number of authors try to comprehend and describe multipolarity as a model, phenomenon, precedent, or possibility.

---

1   Trans: The author uses "IR" to designate the academic field, and "international relations" to designate the relations studied by the field.

The themes of multipolarity, in one way or another, were touched on in the works of David Kampf (in his essay "Emergence of a Multipolar World"),[2] the Yale historian Paul Kennedy (in the book *The Rise and Fall of the Great Empires*),[3] the geopolitician Dale Walton (in the book *Geopolitics and the Great Powers in the 21st Century: Multipolarity and the Revolution in Strategic Perspective*),[4] the American political scientist Dilip Hiro (in the book *After Empire: The Birth of a Multipolar World*)[5] and others. In our opinion, the British IR specialist Fabio Petito came closest to understanding the essence of multipolarity. Petito tried to build a serious and well-grounded alternative to the unipolar world on the basis of the legal and philosophical concepts of Carl Schmitt.[6]

Political actors and influential journalists time and again mention the "multipolar world order" in their speeches and writings. Thus, former US Secretary of State Madeleine Albright, who was the first to call the US "the indispensable nation," announced on February 2, 2000 that the US does not want to "establish and enforce" a unipolar world and that economic integration has already created a "certain world, which can even be called multipolar." On January 26, 2007, a New York Times editorial spoke directly of the "emergence of a multipolar world," together with China, which "takes a parallel place at

---

2   Kampf, David. "The Emergence of a Multipolar World." Foreign Policy. Oct. 20, 2009. http://foreignpolicyblogs.com/2009/10/20/the-emergence-of-a-multipolar-world/.

3   Kennedy, Paul. *The Rise and Fall of the Great Powers.* Unwin Hyman, 1988.

4   Walton, Dale C. *Geopolitics and the Great Powers in the Twenty-first Century. Multipolarity and the Revolution in the Strategic Perspective.* New York:Routledge, 2007.

5   Hiro, Dilip. *After Empire. The Birth of a Multipolar World.* New York: Nation books, 2009.

6   Petito, Fabio. "Dialogue of Civilizations as Global Political Discourse: Some Theoretical Reflections." The Bulletin of the World Public Forum 'Dialogue of Civilizations', vol. 1 no. 2, 21–29. 2004.

the table along with other centers of power, like Brussels or Tokyo."[7] A 2008 US National Intelligence Council report on "Global Tendencies 2025" declares that the rise of a "global multipolar system" should be expected over the next two decades.

In 2009, many considered US President Barack Obama a harbinger of the "era of multipolarity," thinking that he would give priority in American foreign policy to growing centers of power, like Brazil, China, India, and Russia. On July 22, 2009, Vice-President Joe Biden announced during a visit to Ukraine that the US "will try to build a multipolar world."

And yet, in all these books, articles, and pronouncements, there is no precise definition of what a multipolar world (MW) is, nor, all the more so, any sort of systematic and consistent theory of its construction (TMW). Most often, appeal to "multipolarity" implies only an indication that at present, in the process of globalization, in the undisputed center and core of the modern world (the US, Europe, and, more broadly, the 'Global West') certain competitors appear on the horizon, rapidly developing, or simply powerful regional states and blocs of states, belonging to the 'Second' World. Comparison of the potentials of the US and Europe, on one hand, and the growing new centers of power (China, India, Russia, the countries of Latin America, etc.), on the other, convinces more and more of the relativity of the traditional superiority of the West and raises new questions about the logic of the long-term processes determining the global architecture of powers on a planetary scale, in politics, economics, energy, demography, culture, etc.

All of these commentaries and observations are exceedingly important for the construction of the Theory of a Multipolar World, but do not at all compensate for its absence. They should be taken into account in the construction of such a theory; however, it should be

---

7   NYT, Viewpoints: The New Consensus — A Multipolar World.

noted that they are fragments and sketches and fail to rise to the level of even primary theoretical, conceptual generalizations.

Nevertheless, appeal to a multipolar world order can be heard more and more often at official summits, international conferences, and congresses. References to multipolarity are present in a number of important international agreements and in the texts of the conceptions of the national security and defense strategies of many influential, powerful countries (China, Russia, Iran, and in part the European Union). Thus, today as never before, it is necessary to take a step toward beginning the full-fledged elaboration of a theory of a multipolar world in accordance with the basic demands of an academic, scientific approach.

Multipolarity Is Not Congruent with the National, Westphalian Model of Organizing the World

Before we proceed with the construction of a Theory of a Multipolar World (TMW) in earnest, we should strictly delineate the studied conceptual zone. For this, we shall consider the basic concepts and determine the forms of global order that are definitely not multipolar and, accordingly, in regards to which multipolarity is an alternative.

We begin with the Westphalian system, which recognizes the absolute sovereignty of the nation-state and builds on this basis the entire legal field of International Relations. This system, formed after 1648 (the end of the Thirty Years' War in Europe), went through a few stages of its establishment and to one extent or another corresponded to objective reality until the end of the Second World War.

This system was born of the rejection of the pretensions of medieval empires to universalism and a "divine mission," corresponded to bourgeois reforms in European societies, and was based on the position that the highest sovereignty is possessed only by the nation-state, while there is no authority outside it with legal right to interfere in the internal politics of this state, whatever its goals and missions (religious, political, or otherwise). From the middle of the 17th century to the middle of the 20th century, this principle determined European politics and was transferred with certain modifications to the countries of the rest of the world.

The Westphalian system originally concerned only European states, while their colonies were regarded merely as their *extensions*, lacking sufficient political and economic potential to claim independent sovereignty. From the start of the 20th century and during the course of decolonialization, that same Westphalian principle was spread throughout former colonies.

The Westphalian model supposes *full legal equality* among sovereign states. In this model, the world has as many poles of foreign policy decision-making as there are *sovereign states*. This rule implicitly acts even now by inertia, and all international law is based on it. But in practice, of course, there is *inequality* and hierarchical subordination among sovereign states. In the First and Second World Wars the distribution of powers among the largest global powers spilled over into the confrontation of separate blocs, where decisions were made in the country that was most powerful among its allies. As a result of the Second World War, in consequence of the defeat of Nazi Germany and the Axis countries, a bipolar world system of international relations formed in the global system, called the Yalta system. *De jure* international law continued to recognize the absolute sovereignty of any nation-state. *De facto*, however, the major decisions concerning the central questions of the world order and global politics were made *in only two centers*, Washington and Moscow.

A multipolar world differs from the classical Westphalian system in that it does recognize in separate nation-states, legally and formally sovereign, the *status of full-fledged poles*. As a result, the number of poles in a multipolar world should be significantly less than the number of recognized (and unrecognized) nation-states. Today, the great majority of these states cannot by themselves ensure their own security or prosperity in the face of a theoretically possible conflict with the hegemon (the role of which, in our world, is played by the US). Consequently, they are politically and economically *dependent* on external sources. Being dependent, they cannot be centers of real *independent and sovereign will* in global questions of world order.

Multipolarity is not a system of international relations that insists on the *legal* equality of nation-states, considered as matter-of-fact. That is only a facade of an entirely different picture of the world, based on the real, not the nominal, balance of powers and strategic potentials. Multipolarity operates with the state of affairs that exists not only *de jure*, but *de facto*, and it starts from the *principal inequality* of nation-states in the contemporary and empirically fixed world. Moreover, the structure of this inequality is such that secondary and tertiary powers are not able to defend their sovereignty, even in bloc configuration, against a possible external challenge from a hegemonic power. Hence, this sovereignty is today a *legal fiction*.

Multipolarity Is Not Bipolarity

After the Second World War, a bipolar system formed in the world, also called the Yalta system. Formally, it continued to insist on the principle of the absolute sovereignty of all states, and the UN was organized on this principle, continuing the business of the League of Nations. However, in practice there emerged *two* centers of global decision-making: the US and the USSR. The US and the USSR represented two alternative political and economic systems: global capitalism and global socialism. Thus, strategic bipolarity rested on ideological dualism: liberalism versus Marxism.

The bipolar world was based on the economic and military-strategic *parity* of the US and USSR, on the symmetrical comparability of the potential of each of the opposed camps. At the same time, no other country in either camp was even remotely comparable in power to Moscow or Washington. Consequently, there were *two hegemons* on a global scale, which were surrounded by constellations of allied countries (strategically half-vassals). In this model, the national sovereignty of countries, formally recognized, gradually lost its significance. In the first place, every country depended on the global policies of the hegemon to whose sphere of influence it related. So, they were not independent; and regional conflicts (as a rule, in the Third World), quickly grew into the *confrontation of the two superpowers*, which tried to redistribute the balance of planetary influence to "disputed territories." This explains the conflicts in Korea, Vietnam, Angola, Afghanistan, etc.

In the bipolar world, there was also a *third power* — the Non-Aligned Movement. It included a few countries of the Third World that refused to make an unambiguous choice in favour of either capitalism or socialism and preferred to manouevre between the global antagonistic interests of the US and USSR. Some were able to do this to a certain extent, but the very possibility of non-alignment presupposed the presence of precisely two poles, which to one extent or another counterbalanced each other. At the same time, most "non-aligned countries" were in no way able to form a "third pole" since they were isolated, lacking consolidation and a shared socio-economic platform, and inferior in the main respects to the superpowers. The entire world was divided into the capitalist West (the First World, the West), the socialist East (the Second World) and "the rest" (the Third World); what's more, "the rest" was in every sense a *global periphery*, where the interests of the superpowers occasionally came into conflict. Conflict between the superpowers themselves was almost entirely out of the question because of parity (because of mutually assured nuclear destruction). Countries of the periphery (Asia, Africa, Latin America) formed the intermediate zone for the partial reconsideration of the balance of powers.

After the collapse of one of the two poles (the fall of the USSR in 1991), the bipolar system ended. This produced the preconditions for the emergence of an alternative world order. Many analysts and specialists in IR correctly started to speak about the "end of the Yalta system."[8] Recognizing *de jure* sovereignty, *de facto* the Yalta world was built on the principle of the balance of two symmetrical and relatively balanced hegemons. With the exit from the historical arena of one of the hegemons, the entire system ceased to exist. The time of the *unipolar* world order, or "unipolar moment," had come.[9]

The multipolar world is not a bipolar world (as we knew it in the second half of the 20th century), since *today there is no power able by itself to strategically oppose the might of the US and the NATO countries*, and, moreover, no general and clear ideology capable of rallying a significant part of humanity to strict ideational opposition against the ideology of liberal democracy, capitalism, and "human rights," on which the new, this time *sole* hegemony of the US rests. Neither contemporary Russia, nor China, nor India, nor any other state *can, under current circumstances, lay claim by itself to the status of a second pole*. The reestablishment of bipolarity is impossible ideologically (the end of the broad appeal of Marxism), and in terms of the strategic potential and accumulated military-technological resources (for the last thirty years, the US and NATO have pulled so far ahead that no country is capable of symmetrical competition with them militarily, strategically, economically, or technically).

Multipolarity Is Incompatible with a Unipolar World

The collapse of the USSR meant at the same time the disappearance both of a powerful, symmetrical superpower and of an entire gigantic ideological camp. This was *the end of one of the two global hegemons*. The whole structure of the world order from this moment on changed irreversibly and substantially.

At the same time, the remaining pole, led by the US and based on liberal-democratic capitalist ideology, was preserved as a phenomenon

8   Safire, William. "The End of Yalta." *The New York Times*. July 9, 1997.

9   Krauthammer, Ch. "The Unipolar Moment." *Foreign Affairs*. 1990/1991 Winter. Vol. 70, No 1. pp. 23–33.

and continued to expand its sociopolitical system (democracy, the market, the ideology of human rights) on a global scale. This is what is called the *unipolar world*, the unipolar world order. In such a world, there is *a single center of decision-making concerning the fundamental global questions*. The West and its core, the Euro-Atlantic community led by the US, found itself in the role of the sole remaining *hegemon*. Under such circumstances, the entire space of the planet represents a threefold regionalization (described in the neo-Marxist theory of Wallerstein):[10] the area of the core ("the rich North," the "center"), the area of the global periphery ("the poor South," the "periphery"), and the intermediate area (the "semi-periphery," including the big countries rapidly developing capitalistically: China, India, Brazil, a few countries of the Pacific Ocean region, and also Russia, which preserved by inertia a significant strategic, economic, and energy potential).

In the 1990s, the unipolar world seemed to be a reality settled once and for all, and some America analysts pronounced on this basis the thesis of the "end of history" (Fukuyama).[11] This thesis meant that the world is becoming entirely *unipolar* ideologically, politically, economically, and socially, and that henceforth all processes occurring in it would be not a historical drama, based on the battle of ideas and interests, but the economic (and relatively peaceful) competition of economic subjects, analogous to the way in which the domestic politics of free, democratic, liberal regimes runs. Democracy becomes global. On the planet there is only the West and its outskirts, i.e. the countries gradually integrating into it.

The clearest formulation of the theory of unipolarity was offered by American neoconservatives, who emphasized the role of the US in the new global world order, sometimes openly pronouncing America

---

10   Wallerstein, I. *Geopolitics and Geoculture: Essays on the Changing World-System*. Cambridge: Press Syndicate, 1991.

11   Fukuyama, F. *The End of History and the Last Man*.

a "new Empire" (Kaplan)[12] or "beneficent global hegemony" (Kristol, Kagan)[13] and foreseeing the onset of an "American century" (Project for a New American Century).[14] Among neo-conservatives, unipolarity acquired a theoretical foundation. The future world order was seen as an America-centric construction, where the core was the US in the role of the global arbiter and embodiment of the principles of "freedom and democracy," and around this center constellations of other countries are structured, reproducing the American model with varying degrees of precision. They differ according to geography and the extent of their similarity to the US: the near circle — the countries of Europe and Japan; next, the rapidly developing liberal countries of Asia; then everyone else. All of the belts around "global America" in various orbits are included in the processes of "democratization" and "Americanization." The spread of American values occurs alongside the realization of practical American interests and expansion of the area of direct American control on a global scale.

On a strategic level, unipolarity is expressed in the central role of the US in NATO and, in turn, in the asymmetrical superiority of the combined military potential of NATO over all other world powers. At the same time, the West outdoes other non-Western countries in economic potential, technological development, etc. And the most important thing: *precisely the West is the matrix in which the system of values and norms that are today considered a universal standard for all other countries in the world historically formed and was consolidated.* We can call this *global intellectual hegemony,* which, on one hand, serves the technical infrastructure of global control and, on the other, stands at the center of the dominant planetary paradigm. Material

---

12   Kaplan, R.D. *Imperial Grunts: On the Ground with the American Military, from Mongolia to the Philippines to Iraq and Beyond.* New York: Vintage, 2006.

13   Fukuyama, Francis. "After Neoconservatism" *The New York Times Magazine.* February 19, 2006.

14   http://www.newamericancentury.org/.

hegemony goes hand in hand with spiritual, intellectual, cognitive, cultural, informational hegemony.

In principle, the American political elite rules precisely in such a consciously hegemonic manner; however, the neoconservatives speak about this openly and transparently, while representatives of other political and ideational tendencies prefer more indirect expressions. Even critics of the unipolar world in the US itself do not call into question the "universality" of American values and the striving to assert them on a global scale. Objections focus on the question of how realistic this project is in the middle- to long-term perspective and whether the US will be able by itself to carry the burden of a global empire. The problems on the path to such a direct, open American domination, which seemed to be a realized fact in the 1990s, led some American analysts (including Krauthammer, who introduced the term) to speak of the end of the "unipolar moment."[15] But despite everything, precisely *unipolarity* in one or another form — open or concealed — is the model of world order that became *reality* after 1991 and remains so even today.

Unipolarity Is Accompanied in Practice by the Nominal Preservation of the Westphalian System and with the Inertial Remnants of the Bipolar World

As before, the sovereignty of all nation-states is recognized *de jure;* the UN Security Council partially still reflects the balance of powers corresponding to the realities of the "Cold War."

Accordingly, American unipolar hegemony *de facto* exists simultaneously with a number of international institutions expressing the balance of power of other eras and cycles in the history of international relations. The contradictions between the *de facto* and *de jure* states of affairs constantly make themselves known, in part in the acts of

---

15 Krauthammer, Charles. "The Unipolar Moment Revisited." *National Interest,* volume 70, pp. 5–17. Winter 2002.

direct intervention by the US or Western coalitions in sovereign states (sometimes bypassing Security Council vetoes of similar acts). In such cases, as the US invasion of Iraq in 2003, we also see an example of the unilateral violation of the principle of the sovereignty of independent states (ignoring the Westphalian model), and refusal to take into account Russia's position (Putin's position) in the UN Security Council, and even Washington's inattention toward the protests of European NATO partners (Chirac in France, Schröder in Germany).

The most consistent supporters of unipolarity (for instance, Republican John McCain) insist on establishing a world order that corresponds to the real balance of power. They suggest the creation, in place of the UN, of a different model, a "League of Democracies,"[16] in which the dominant positions of the US, i.e., unipolarity, would be secured *legally*. Such a project of the legalization in the structure of international relations of a unipolar world and the hegemonic status of the "American empire" is one of the possible directions of evolution of the global political system. It is entirely obvious that a multipolar world order does not simply differ from a unipolar one but is its direct *antithesis*. Unipolarity proposes *one* hegemon and one center of decision-making; multipolarity insists on *several centers*, such that none has the exclusive right and must take into account the positions of the others. *Multipolarity is thus a direct logical alternative to unipolarity.* There can be no compromise between them: according to the rules of logic, *the world is either unipolar or multipolar.* At the same time, what matters is not how one or another model is legally formulated, but how it is *de facto*. In the Cold War, diplomats and politicians reluctantly acknowledged bipolarity, which was nevertheless an obvious fact. So, we should distinguish between diplomatic language and concrete reality. Today's world order is *in fact* arranged as a unipolar world. We can only argue about whether this is good or bad, whether it is daybreak or sundown, whether it will last long or end quickly.

---

16 McCain, John. "America Must Be a Good Role Model." *The Financial Times*, March 18, 2008.

But the fact remains a fact. *We live in a unipolar world.* The unipolar moment continues (although some analysts assert that it is already coming to an end).

The Multipolar World Is Not Non-Polar

American critics of strict unipolarity, and especially the ideological rivals of the neoconservatives centered in the Council on Foreign Relations, proposed a different term instead of unipolarity, *nonpolarity*.[17] This concept is built on the idea that processes of globalization will develop even further, and the Western model of world order will broaden its presence to all countries and peoples of the world. In this way, the intellectual and value hegemony of the West will continue. The global world will be a world of liberalism, democracy, the free market, and human rights. But the role of the US as a *national* power and leader of globalization will, according to supporters of this theory, be reduced. Instead of direct American hegemony, the model of "global governance" will take shape, in which will participate the representatives of various countries in solidarity with the general values and moving toward the establishment of a single sociopolitical space worldwide. We are dealing here again with an analogue to the "end of history" (Fukuyama), only described in other terms. The non-polar world will be based implicitly on the cooperation of democratic countries. But gradually, in the process of establishment other non-state actors should be included: NGOs, social movements, separate civil groups, network societies, etc. The major practice in the establishment of a non-polar world is scattering the level of decision-making from one authority (today, Washington) to many on a lower level, right up to online planetary referenda concerning important events and the actions of all humanity. Economics replaces politics, and market competition sweeps aside all national borders. Security is

---

17 Haass, Richard N. "The Age of Nonpolarity.—What Will Follow U.S. Dominance." *Foreign Affairs.* May/June 2008.

transformed from a state matter to a matter for citizens themselves. The era of *global democracy* sets in.

In its general features, this theory agrees with globalization and is thought of as a stage that must replace the unipolar world. But only under the *condition* that the sociopolitical, value-based, techno-logical, and economic model (liberal democracy), advanced today by the US and the West, will become a *universal phenomenon*, and the need for a strong defense of democratic and liberal ideals by the US will fall away: all regimes opposing the West, democratization, and Americanization will be destroyed before the onset of the non-polar world. The elites of all countries should be homogeneously capitalis-tic, liberal, and democratic — in a word, "Western," regardless of their historical, geographic, religious, and national origin.

The project of a non-polar world is supported by many very in-fluential political and financial groups, from the Rothschilds to Soros and his fund.

The project of a non-polar world is directed toward the future. It is thought of as the global formation that should *replace* unipolarity; as that which follows it. It is not so much an alternative as a *continuation*. And this continuation becomes possible only to the extent that the center of gravity in society will shift from today's combination of the alliance of two levels of hegemony — *material* (the American military-industrial complex, the Western economy and resources) and *spiritual* (norms, procedures, values) — *to a purely intellectual hegemony*, while the significance of material domination will gradually abate. This is the *global information society*, where the main governance will de-velop in the sphere of reason, through rule over intellects, control over consciousness, and the programming of a virtual world.

The unipolar world in no way coincides with the project of a non-polar world, since it accepts neither the validity of the unipolar moment as a prelude to a future world order, nor the intellectual hegemony of the West, nor the universality of its values, nor the dif-fusion of the level of decision-making onto a planetary multitude, without taking into account their cultural and civilizational identities. The non-polar world proposes that the American model of the melting pot be spread throughout the world. As a result, all differences between peoples and nations will be erased, and individualized, atomized humanity will become a cosmopolitan "civil society" without borders. Multipolarity thinks that the centers of decision-making should remain on a rather high level (but not in one place, as today in a unipolar world) and that the cultural peculiarities of each concrete civilization should be preserved and strengthened (not dissolved into a single cosmopolitan multitude).

Multipolarity Is Not Multilateralism

Another model of world order, distancing itself somewhat from direct American hegemony, is *multilateralism*. This concept is widespread in the American Democratic Party; formally, President Barack Obama followed precisely this model in his foreign policy. In the context of American foreign policy debates, this approach contrasts with the unipolarity insisted on by neoconservatives.

Multilateralism means in practice that the US should not act in the domain of international relations wholly and fully relying solely on its own forces and informing all its allies and "vassals" in an imperialistic manner. Instead, Washington should take into account the positions of its partners, argue for and convince others of decisions in dialogue with them, attract them to its side with rational conclusions and sometimes compromises. In such a case, the US should be "first among equals," not a "dictator among subordinates." This obligates the US to its allies in certain ways in foreign policy and demands submission to a shared strategy. This general strategy is in the current case *the strategy of the West to establish a global democracy, market, and the implementation of the ideology of human rights on a planetary scale.* But in this process, the US, as leader, should not directly equate its national interests with the "universal" values of Western civilization, in whose name it acts. In certain cases it is preferable to act in a coalition, and sometimes even to concede something to partners.

Multilateralism differs from unipolarity in that the emphasis is placed here on the West as a whole, and especially on its "value" (i.e. normative) aspect. In this respect, the apologists for multilateralism resemble those who support a non-polar world. The difference between multilateralism and non-polarity consists only in the fact that multilateralism emphasizes coordination among democratic Western countries, while non-polarity includes as actors also *non-state* players: NGOs, networks, social movements, etc.

It is significant that in practice Obama's multilateral policies, announced by him and by Secretary of State Hillary Clinton, differed little from the direct and transparent imperialism of George W. Bush, in whose administration the neoconservatives dominated. US military interventions continue (Libya), and American troops kept their presence in occupied Afghanistan and Iraq.

A multipolar world does not coincide with a multilateral world order, since it does not agree to the universalism of Western values and does not recognize the right of countries of the 'rich North'—neither alone nor collectively—to act in the name of all humanity and to act (even compositely) as the sole center of decision-making concerning the most significant questions.

Summary

Delineating the meaning of the concept of "multipolarity" through a chain of juxtaposed or alternative terms outlines the semantic field in which we will have to proceed to build our theory of multipolarity. Until now, we have spoken only of what multipolarity *is not*. These negations and distinctions allow us to distinguish by contrast a number of constitutive and rather *positive* characteristics. If we summarize the second, positive part, emerging from the series of differentiations we made, we get approximately the following picture:

1. The multipolar world is a *radical alternative to the unipolar world* (existing in fact today), in that it insists on the presence of *several* independent and sovereign centers of global, strategic decision-making on a planetary level;

2. These centers should be sufficiently equipped and independent *materially* to have the possibility to defend their sovereignty on a material level in the face of the invasion of a probable enemy, as a model of which we can take the most powerful force in the world today. This demand amounts to the possibility to *oppose the material, military, strategic hegemony of the US and NATO*;

3. These centers of decision-making are not obligated to recognize as a *sine qua non* Western norms and values (democracy, liberalism, the free market, parliamentarism, human rights, individualism, cosmopolitanism, etc.) and can be *entirely independent of the spiritual hegemony of the West*;

4. The multipolar world *does not propose a return to a bipolar system*, since today there exists neither strategically nor ideologically a force capable of opposing alone the material and spiritual hegemony of the contemporary West and its leader, the US. There must be *more than two* poles in a multipolar world.

5. The multipolar world does not consider serious the sovereignty of existing nation-states, so long as it is declared on a purely legal level and is not confirmed by the presence of sufficient military, strategic, economic, and political potential. To be a sovereign subject in the 21st century, the nation-state is no longer enough. *Under these circumstances, only an aggregate or coalition of states can have real sovereignty.* The Westphalian system, continuing to exist *de jure*, no longer reflects the real system of international relations and should be reconsidered.

6. *Multipolarity is irreducible to non-polarity and to multilateralism*, since it does not locate the center of decision-making (pole) in the

authority of a world government, nor in the club of the US and
its democratic allies ("the global West"), nor in the supranational
level of networks, NGOs, and other civil society actors. A pole
must be located *somewhere else.*

These six points set the stage for further elaborations and conceptually
embody the main features of multipolarity. However, this description,
although it substantially advances our understanding of the essence of
multipolarity, is not yet enough to claim the status of a theory. It is a
first step, with which full-fledged theorization only begins.

Today there is no ready Theory of a Multipolar World in any of the
available paradigms [of International Relations], nor, all the more so,
is there even a place reserved for such a theory. For a long time, the
field of International Relations was considered an "American science,"
since it developed primarily in the US. But in recent decades it has
become studied more widely in scientific establishments and institutions worldwide. However, the discipline still carries a clear mark of
West-centrism. It was developed in Western countries in the era of
Modernity and preserves historical and geographical ties with the
context in which it originally arose and where it was established. This
is expressed in particular in the main axis of debates, around which
IR formed as a discipline (realists versus liberals), which reflected the
specific nature of the particular worries and problems of precisely
American foreign policy (repeating in certain ways the classic US
argument between isolationists and expansionists). In the latest phase,
and especially in the sphere of postpositivist approaches, tendencies
have clearly arisen of *relativizing America-centrism* (West-centrism
generally). Impulses toward the democratization of theories and
methods, the broadening of criteria, and the more uniform spread
of actors in IR have made themselves known, as has a more attentive
("thick") analysis of their semantic structures and identities. This is a
step towards the relativization of Western epistemic hegemony. But
to the present even *the critique of Western hegemony has proceeded*

according to the laws of that very hegemony. Thus, typical Western concepts of democracy and democratization, freedom and equality, are transferred to non-Western societies and are sometimes even opposed to the West, as though these concepts are "something universal."[18] If opposition to the West proceeds under the banners of the universalism of Western values, this opposition is doomed to be sterile.

Thus, in order to leave the borders of West-centric civilization, it is necessary to stand at a distance from all its theoretical concepts and methodological strategies, even those that comprise critique of the West. In reality, an alternative model of IR and, accordingly, an alternative structure of world order can take shape only *in opposition to the entire spectrum of Western theories in IR* — in the first place positivist, but in part also postpositivist ones.

The absence among the IR theorists, who we have considered, of a Theory of a Multipolar World (TMW) proves to be not an annoying accident or sign of neglect, but an entirely lawlike fact: it simply cannot exist in this context, somehow or other encoded with the attitudes of Western cognitive (epistemological) hegemony. Nevertheless, theoretically it can full well be constructed. And taking account of the broad panorama of existing IR theories will only help to formulate it correctly.

If we seriously start building such a theory and take a distance at the outset from the cognitive hegemony of the West in the sphere of IR, that is, if we call into question the existing spectrum of IR theories as an axiomatic base, then at the second stage we can borrow separate elements from that sphere, each time stipulating in detail on what terms and in what context we do this. No existing IR theory, strictly speaking, is relevant for the construction of a Theory of a Multipolar World. But many of them contain elements that, on the contrary, can well be integrated into a TMW under certain circumstances.

---

18 Sen, Amartya. "Democracy as a Universal Value." *Journal of Democracy.* October 3, 1999.

2

Hegemony and its Deconstruction

The Meaning of Postpositivism

THE CONSTRUCTION OF a Theory of a Multipolar World begins with a deep historico-philosophical analysis of the very discipline of IR. Most useful in this case are *postpositivist theories*, which strive (though most often unsucessfully) to transcend the limits of "ethnocentrism"[1] characteristic of Western European culture, science, and politics and to deconstruct the will to power and domination of the West (in the most recent period of history, of the US) as the main content of the entire theoretical discourse in this field.[2] Representatives of critical theory and postmodernity in IR, and to no less extent supporters of the historico-sociological approach and normativism, readily demonstrate that all contemporary theories of IR are built *around a hegemonic discourse*.[3] This hegemonic discourse is a characteristic feature of Western European civilization, with its roots

---

1   Sumner, W. *Folkways*. Boston: Ginn, 1907.
2   Hobson, J. M. *The Eurocentric Conception of World Politics: Western International Theory, 1760–2010*.
3   Ibid.

in the Greco-Roman idea of the structure of the *ecumene*, with a core of "civilization" and "culture" and peripheral zones of "barbarism" and "savagery." Other empires also had such an idea: the Persian, Egyptian, Babylonian, Chinese, and also Indian civilizations invariably considered themselves the "center of the world," the "Middle Kingdom."

On a narrower level, we encounter a similar "ethnocentric" approach among practically all archaic tribes and collectives, which operate with a map of cultural geography in the center of which is the tribe itself (people), while around it, according to distance, is the external world, gradually dehumanizing, right up to the "other-world," spirits, monsters, and other mythical entities.

We can trace the genealogy of contemporary Western universalism back to the era of medieval empires and even further to ancient Greco-Roman civilization, and, finally, to the archaic ethnocentrism of the simplest human collectives, archaic tribes, hordes. Everywhere, even the most undeveloped primitive tribes consider themselves "people" and even the "highest beings," and refuse this status to their closest neighbours, even when these neighbours obviously demonstrate social and technological skills far superior to the culture of the given tribe. Postpositivists interpret this as a *basic cognitive attitude*, which *a posteriori* selectively finds (or fabricates, if they're absent) biased arguments affirming this imagined "superiority" and "universalism."

Contra-Hegemony

The exposure of Western hegemony as the basis of Western discourse, the placement of this discourse in a concrete historical and geographical context, is the first fundamental step toward the construction of a Theory of a Multipolar World. Multipolarity will become actual only if it is able to carry out a *deconstruction of hegemony* and discredit the pretensions of the West to the universalism of its values, systems, methods, and philosophical foundations. If it is not possible to overthrow the hegemony, any "multipolar" models will only be variants of West-centric theories. Those who, belonging to Western intellectual culture, strive to transcend the limits of hegemony and create a contra-hegemonic discourse (Cox, for instance) remain fatefully within this hegemony, since they build their critique on such postulates as "democracy," "freedom," "equality," "justice," "human rights," etc., which, in turn, are a set of *West-centric* concepts of the world. Ethnocentrism is contained in their very foundations. They mark out the true path, but are themselves unable to follow it to the end. They understand the artificiality and falsity of the pretensions of their civilization to universality, but cannot find access to alternative civilizational structures. Thus, contra-hegemonic theory must be built *outside* the Western semantic field, in an intermediate area, between the "core" of the world-system (in Wallerstein's terminology) and the "periphery" (where according to cultural circumstances a correct understanding of Western hegemony is so unlikely that it can be disregarded). The "Second World," in turn, precisely because of its engagement in a constant and intense dialogue with the West, can, on one hand, recognize the nature and structure of hegemony and, on the other, has in its sources alternative systems of cultural values and basic civilizational criteria, on which it can rely on rejecting this hegemony. In other words, contra-hegemony in the intellectual space of the West itself must always remain *abstract*, while in the area of the "Second World" it can become *concrete*.

Deconstructing the Will to Power

The first stage requires fixing attention on the will to power of the West as a civilization.

Today the West pretends to the universality and absoluteness of its value system and presents itself as something *global*. On the basis of that system it strives to reorganize the entire world, spreading throughout it the procedures, criteria, norms, and codes that were worked out by the West in the last hundred years. As we saw, identifying a local culture with a universal culture and a limited collective with all of humanity (or at least with the chosen part of humanity, its elite, capable of acting in its name) is a characteristic feature of *any socius*, whether imperial or archaic. Thus, the very claim of Western civilization to universality is nothing unique. Ethnocentrism, dividing the world into a "we-group" (as a rule, we are "good, normative, models") and a "they-group" (as a rule, they are "bad, hostile, threatening") is a social constant.[4] And at the same time the evident arbitrariness and relativity of such an attitude is rarely ever reflected on and is insufficiently reflected on by even the most developed and complex societies, demonstrating in other questions flexibility of judgment and skills of apperception. *The will to power moves societies, but industriously avoids directly glancing at itself.* It strives to conceal itself behind "appearances" or a complex system of argumentation.

We must begin the construction of a TMW by *acknowledging the West as the core of hegemony and setting this down as a clear and unequivocal axiom.* As soon as we try to do this, we are at once met with the intensive objections of Western intellectuals. This reproach, they will say, is correct with respect to the European past. But at present Western culture itself rejected colonial practices and Eurocentric theories and adopted the norms of democracy and multiculturalism. In order to respond to this, one can momentarily take a Marxist stance and demonstrate that the West in the bourgeois era identified its fate with capital and become the area of its geographical fixation. But the point of capital consists in domination over the proletariat, so under the mask of "democracy" and "equality" under the conditions of capitalism there are concealed that same will to power and practices of exploitation and violence. That is how representatives of Critical Theory respond, and they are absolutely right. But in order not to be attached to Marxism, with its additional burdensome dogmas, many of which are far from evident and unacceptable, *it is necessary to expand the*

---

4 Sumner, W. *Folkways*. Boston: Ginn, 1907.

theoretical base of the unmasking of hegemony and to transfer it from a
socio-economic to a more general, civilizational-cultural context.

The Eurasian Critique of Eurocentrism and Western Universalism

Russian Slavophiles undertook a detailed criticism of the hegemonic pretensions of Western civilization, which was continued in the 20th century by Eurasianists. Prince Trubetskoy, in his work *Europe and Humanity*, laid the foundation for the ideational stream of Eurasianism, brilliantly showing the artificial and unfounded pretensions of the West to universalism through philosophical, culturological, and sociological analysis. In particular, he pointed to the glaring inadequacy of similar methods, like the reduction of the content of the fundamental tome *The Pure Theory of Law* by the jurist Hans Kelsen almost exclusively to the history of Roman Law and European jurisprudence, as though other legal systems (Persian, Chinese, Hindu, etc.) simply did not exist.[5] The equal sign between "European" and "universal" is an unjustified pretension. Its sole basis is the fact of direct physical power and technological superiorty, *the right of might*. But this right of might is limited to the domain in which operate laws of material comparison and juxtaposition. The transfer of these markers to the intellectual, spiritual sphere is a variety of "racism" and "ethnocentrism."

Starting from these principles, Eurasianists developed the theory of the plurality of historico-cultural types (the foundations of which were laid by Danilevsky), among which the modern Western type (Greco-Roman civilization) is only a *geographical locality* and *historical episode*. Hegemony and the success of its imposition on others is a fact that cannot be left out of account. But, recognized for what it is, it ceases to be "obvious" or "fate" and becomes only a discourse, a

---

5   Kelsen, H. *Reine Rechtslehre*. Vienna, 1934.

process, a manufactured and subjective phenomenon, which one can accept or reject, admit or contest.

Thus, contra-hegemony, the necessity for which is justified by supporters of critical theory in IR, can be successfully supplemented by an entirely different intellectual arsenal, from the side of conservative Eurasianists, oriented in their opposition to the West not toward the "proletariat" and "equality," but toward culture, tradition, and spiritual values.

The Historical Metamorphoses of Hegemony

Next, it is important to trace the *metamorphoses* that Western hegemony has undergone in the last century.

When we are dealing with traditional states or empires, the will to power is expressed more *distinctly and transparently*. That's how it was in the period of the empire of Alexander of Macedon, the Roman Empire, the medieval Holy Roman Empire of the German Nation, etc. But at the basis of later imperial universalism there was first Greek philosophy and culture, then Roman Law, and later the Christian Church. In these stages, the West's will to power took the form of a hierarchical estate society and imperial strategies in relations with neighbouring peoples, who were either included in the Western *ecumene* or, if this could not be accomplished, became enemies to be defended against. Power relations and structures of domination were transparent in both domestic and foreign politics. The peculiar features of such an "international system" are studied in detail by Buzan and Little, who define it as "ancient" or "classical."[6] Here, hegemony is undisguised and frank, and, consequently, it is not "hegemony" in the full sense, as Gramsci understood it, since domination is here realized explicitly even by those subject to it. Clear power can either be suffered

---

6   Buzan, B. and Little, R. *International Systems in World History*. Oxford: Oxford
     University Press, 2010.

or, given the opportunity and the desire, overthrown. Everything is more complicated with hegemony (in the Gramscian sense).

Hegemony as such takes shape in modernity, when the entire "international system" changes from the "classical" to the "global" (Buzan and Little). The West enters modernity and henceforth radically changes the basis of its universalism and the formulation of its will to power. Henceforth, this goes under the name of "Enlightenment," "progress," "science," "secularism," and "reason," and also as the struggle against "prejudices" of the past in the name of a "better future" and "human freedom." In this period, nation-states and the first bourgeois-democratic regimes are formed. And although this period of history knows the horrible practices of slave-trading and colonization, as well as bloody wars between "enlightened" European countries themselves, it is customary to believe that humanity (=West) entered a new era and is gradually moving toward "progress," "freedom," and "equality." The open imperial will to power and the concept of the "Christian Ecumene" are transformed into new ideals, summed up in the concept of "progress." Henceforth "progress" is taken as a universal value, and in its name new forms of domination unfold. Postmodernists in IR show this wonderfully, interpreting the technological ascent of Western civilization in modernity as a new expression of the will to power, changing, however, its structure. Now, hierarchical relations are established not between "Christians" and "barbarians," but between "progressive" and "backward" societies and peoples, between "contemporary society" and "traditional society." The level of technological development becomes the criterion for assigning roles in the hierarchy: developed countries become "masters," undeveloped countries, "slaves."

In the first stage of modernity this new structure of inequality is expressed crudely in the practice of colonialization. Later it is preserved in more subtle forms. In any case, the "global system" of IR, reflecting the basic attitudes of modernity, is a purely hegemonic order, where the West is the hegemon, pretending to full control, both strategic and cognitive. It is at once the dictatorship of Western *technique* and Western *mentality*. Accordingly, the social markers of Western society in modernity and its values are regarded as obligatory for all other peoples and cultures. And whatever differs from this system is looked at with suspicion, as something "underdeveloped," "under-Western." Essentially, this is the transfer of the theory of the "subhuman" from a *biological* (as in German racists who were, incidentally, products of European modernity, as Arendt shows) to a *cultural* level.

The Rejection of Neoliberalism and Globalism

In the sphere of IR theories, realism and liberalism are striking expressions of conceptual hegemony. They build all their concepts on the basis of the implied universalism of the West and its values (and also interests) and, accordingly, secure and actively support the hegemonic order.

On another level, the unipolar model and multilateral approach, and even global non-polarity, are also variant formulations of hegemony, both direct and open ("unipolarity" and the "soft version," multilateralism) and implicit and subtle (since globalization, the transnationalism of neoliberals, and constructivist projects are also forms of the expansion of the Western code to the entire planet).

Thus, the elaboration of a Theory of a Multipolar World must pass through the rejection of the very foundations of Western hegemony, and, accordingly, the IR theories built thereupon.

The Critique of Marxism (Eurocentrism)

Things are more complex with the Marxist theory of IR. On one hand, it harshly criticizes hegemony itself, interpreting it as a form of domination intrinsic to capitalism. In this, it is most relevant and productive. But on the other hand, it starts from the same universal and eurocentric ideas of modernity, like "progress," "development," "democracy," "equality," etc., which inserts it into the general context of a precisely *Western* discourse. Even if Marxists are in solidarity with the independence movements of Third World peoples and of non-Western countries on the whole against Western dominance, they foresee for these countries a universal development scenario that repeats the path of Western societies and do not permit thoughts about the very possibility of some other logic of history. Marxists support non-Western peoples in their anti-colonial struggles, in order for them to *more quickly* pass independently through all stages of the Western path of development and build a society essentially like Western societies.[7] All societies must pass through the phase of capitalism, their classes must become fully internationalized, and *only then* will the conditions for a world revolution be ripe. These aspects of Marxism in IR contradict the Theory of a Multipolar World in the following ways:

- they are based on the same Western universalism;

- they acknowledge a unidirectional vector of history for all societies;

- they indirectly justify capitalism and the bourgeois order, considering it a necessary phase of social development, without the coming of which neither revolution nor world communism are possible.

In this case, Marxism is the *opposite side of Western hegemony*, which, while critiquing its more odious and false aspects and discovering its class essence, at the same time does not call into question the *historical justifiedness and even inexorableness* of this order of things. Marxists and supporters of the World-Systems Theory think that Western hegemony is loathsome but inevitable, and that to fight against it directly is pointless, since this only *defers* its inevitable victory on a global scale and, accordingly, *postpones* the moment of world revolution. Thus, the

---

7   *The Eurocentric Conception of World Politics: Western International Theory, 1760–2010.*

Marxist school in IR should be looked at not as the antithesis of hegemony, but as its paradoxical *invariant*, which does not lack a certain
methodological and conceptual value.

The Critique of Universalism in the Postpositivist IR Theories

Closest of all to a Theory of a Multipolar World are *postpositivist theories*, which criticize modernity as such and sometimes rise to a direct
and general anti-Western attack on hegemony and the will to power
that is its main component. Among such theories, the most interesting are those that in the course of deconstructing Western hegemony
clearly place the West in spatio-geographic borders and, correspondingly, trace the evolution of Western domination both temporally and
spatially. At the same time, they carry out an epistemological analysis
of intellectual concepts and schemas that at each historical stage formulated the Western will to power and justified its hegemony. Such
works show that the West is a civilization among other civilizations,
and as such its pretensions to univeralism reduce to the level of concrete historical and geographic borders. In this sense "contemporary
society" and all the axiomatic theses connected with it (secularism,
anthropocentrism, the importance of technology, pragmatism, hedonism, individualism, materialism, consumerism, transparency, tolerance, democracy, liberalism, parliamentarism, freedom of speech,
etc.) are something *local and transitory*, not more than a *moment* of
world history, with strict limits. Such an analysis undermines the
main condition of Western hegemony, its concealed universalist pretensions, advanced as something "obvious and self-evident." This is
the tremendous contribution of the postpositivists to the elaboration
of a Theory of a Multipolar World. But here we must raise a question
(perhaps a rhetorical one): why has a completed theory of multipolarity not taken shape among postpositivists, if the relativization of the
West and the deconstruction of its hegemony were so much in the

fore and, it would seem, themselves urged toward turning to other civilizations and other poles, and then on the basis of a deep analysis of these civilizational alternatives to offer a polycentric picture of the world? But postpositivists, as a rule, only bring to their *logical limits* precisely West-centric discourse, proposing to make *not a step in the direction* away from the West and modernity, but *a step forward*, into posthistory, into the world that should follow exhausted modernity, but which maintains succession with it, a logical, historical, and moral connection. Instead of subjecting to deconstruction the principles of "freedom," "democracy," "equality," etc., postmodernists insist only on "more freedom," "real democracy," and "full equality," and criticize modernity for failing to deliver these. Hence arise the arguments among numerous contemporary philosophers and sociologists over whether postmodernism can be considered a truly new and alternative paradigm in comparison with modernity, or whether we are dealing merely with high modernity, ultra-modernity, a "new modernity," i.e. with the presuppositions and norms, emphasized but not realized, of modernity, carried out to their logical conclusion.

Regardless, despite their unequaled merits and the usefulness of their works for the construction of a Theory of a Multipolar World, postpositivists remain deeply *Western people* (whoever they might be by origin) and they continue to think and act within the framework of Western civilization, a part of which they are, even when they are desperately critiquing it and its foundations (we have to notice that invitation to rational criticism is a value in the very model of modernity). Postmodernists *clear the path* for the construction of a Theory of a Multipolar World, since thanks to their works the hegemony of the West becomes an obvious, transparent, and comprehensively described phenomenon, and the pretensions of Western values to universalism are explained through appeal to precisely this hegemony and are its practical consequences. This means that it is exposed and ceases to be as effective as when its presence is neither recognized nor noticed. Western values and attitudes are locally and historically limited, not global and invariant; accordingly, the world order built on their basis is the expression of hegemonic domination and the product of the expansion of one center in mental and ideational spheres, not fate, not progress, not an objective law of development and preordained destiny. Having asserted and shown this, we find ourselves *face to face* with hegemony. It no longer penetrates us gradually, saturating us and seizing control over our will and consciousness. It is objectified as an external, foreign power, separate from us and trying to impose itself on us through suggestion and the application of its absolute power. Looking at hegemony even once eye to eye, we will never be the same.

Civilization as Actor: Large Space and *Politeia*

Huntington's Theory: The Introduction of the Concept of Civilization

DESPITE THE GREAT significance of postpositivist IR theories, not they, but a representative of the conservative movement in American politics, the realist political philosopher Samuel Huntington, came closest to a TMW. In his article and later polemical book "The Clash of Civilizations," he developed a conceptual picture of the balance of power in the contemporary world that can full well be taken as a sketch of a TMW in its first approximation.

In the work that made him world famous and provoked a squall of reaction, Huntington examines the new conditions of the world order that followed the collapse of the bipolar world. He polemicizes against his student, another famous political analyst, Fukuyama, who, interpreting the end of the bipolar world, came to the conclusion of the "end of history," i.e. the factual worldwide triumph of the liberal-democratic model and globalization. In the spirit of the neoliberal paradigm of IR, Fukuyama thought that:

- democracy had become a universal norm for the whole world, and thus,

- henceforth the threat of military conflicts would be minimized (if not excluded altogether, since "democracies do not fight democracies"),

- global economic competition is becoming the sole norm,

- civil society was approved instead of nation-states,

- the time is coming to proclaim a world government.

Huntington responds to this with pessimistic positions. According to him,

- the end of the bipolar world does not lead automatically to the establishment of a global and homogeneous liberal-democratic world order, and, in consequence,

- history has not ended, and,

- it is premature to speak of the end of conflicts and wars.

We have ceased to be bipolar, but have not become global or unipolar. An entirely new configuration has been laid down, with new collisions, new clashes, tensions, and conflicts. Here, Huntington approaches the most important point and advances an absolutely fundamental and still underappreciated hypothesis concerning the question *who will be the actor of this future world*. He names as this actor *civilizations*.

Precisely this conceptual step should be regarded as the start of the emergence of an entirely new theory, a Theory of a Multipolar World. Huntington accomplishes the most important thing, he distinguishes a new actor, civilization, and simultaneously speaks of a plurality of actors, using in the title of his article the plural form of this word, the clash of "*civilizations*."

If we agree with Huntington on this principal point, we will find ourselves in a conceptual field that transcends the limits of the classical theories of IR and even the postpositivist paradigms. We have only to recognize the plurality of civilizations and to identify them as the main actors (units) in the new system of international relations to get a first approximation of a ready *map of a multipolar world*. Now, we have identified what a pole is in this multipolar order: *the pole is the civilization*. Consequently, we can answer at once the fundamental question about how many poles a multipolar world must have. The answer: *as many as there are civilizations*.

Thus, thanks to Huntington, we get as a first approximation a frame for the new theory. This theory postulates a model in which there are a several *centers* of global decision-making in the field of international relations, and these centers are the corresponding civilizations.

Huntington belongs historically to the realist school of IR. Hence, he moves at once from distinguishing civilizations as actors of the new world order to an analysis of the probability of conflicts (clashes) among them. The basic realist model is built in the same way in evaluating national interests: in the first place, in their analysis of international relations they consider the probability of conflicts, the area of clashing interests, and the possibility of ensuring defense and security. But the fundamental difference is that classical realists apply these criteria to nation-states, taken as the main and sole actors in international relations, as a strict, legally constituted reality, internationally recognized, while Huntington applies the same approach to civilizations, a less distinct and conceptually elaborated concept. Nevertheless, precisely Huntington's intuition and the qualitative shift toward the definition of the actor of the new world order from the nation-state to the civilization is the most important aspect of his theory. It opens entirely new paths to understanding the structure of international relations and lays the foundations for a TMW.

The Concept of "Civilization" in IR

Here, it is important to understand *what a civilization is* and what this term, fundamental for the TMW, means.

Civilization is not a concept that figures in any IR theory, whether positivist or postpositivist. It is not the state, not the political regime, not the class, not a network, not a society [*soobshchestvo*], not a group of individuals, and not separate individuals. *A civilization is a collective community [obshchnost'], united by belonging to the same spiritual, historical, cultural, mental, and symbolic traditions (most often religious in its roots, though not necessarily realized in terms of a concrete religion), the members of which sense intimacy toward one another, regardless of national, class, political, or ideological belonging.*

After Spengler's classic work, some authors, following him, distinguish "civilization" and "culture," whereby "culture" is understood as a spiritual-intellectual community, and by "civilization" rational-technological arrangements and structures. According to Spengler, a civilization is a "cooled off" culture, a culture that has lost its inner forces and will to development and flourishing and sunk to alienated mechanical forms. However, this distinction did not become generally accepted, and in the majority of works (Toynbee's, for instance) the concepts of "civilization" and "culture" are practically synonymous. For us it is important that Huntington understands by "civilization" practically the same thing as "culture," and so it is no mistake that in describing and enumerating civilizations, he appeals predominantly to religions and religious systems.

In the theoretical field of IR, this concept is raised for the first time and is only now positioned as a potential actor of global politics. According to Buzan and Little's classification:

- in a *classic* or *ancient* system of international relations (traditional societies, pre-modernity), traditional states and empires are the main actors;

- in a *global* system (international relations in modernity), bourgeois nation-states are;

- in the most recent *postmodern* system, alongside traditional states, network societies, asymmetrical groups, and other "multitudes" are.

None of them have civilizations as actors. "Civilization" as a concept figures in historical science, in sociology, and in culturology. But in IR, the concept is introduced for the first time.

Huntington's logic, advancing the hypothesis of civilizations in IR, is fairly transparent. The end of the bipolar world and confrontation of two ideological camps, the capitalistic and socialistic, ends with the victory of capitalism and the fall of the USSR. Henceforth, the capitalist West no longer has a "formal" adversary capable of justifying its position on a rational and intellectual level, offering a symmetrical alternative world system, and proving in practice its competitiveness. Fukuyama hurriedly concludes from this that the West has become a global phenomenon, and all countries and societies of the world have become a single homogeneous field, reproducing with slight differences parliamentary democracy, the market economy, and the ideology of human rights. Thus, for Fukuyama, the time of nation-states has passed, and the world stands on the verge of full and final integration. Humanity is being transformed before our eyes into global civil society, politics is giving way to economics, war is being replaced entirely by trade, liberal ideology is becoming a universally recognized norm without alternatives, and all peoples and cultures are mixing in a single cosmopolitan melting pot.

In this case, Fukuyama followed the rules of "thin" analysis. He entirely correctly distinguishes the main and most striking features of the events that were happening. Indeed, the end of socialism disposes of the historical arena of the most serious and impressive ideological adversary of liberal democracy, making the latter "universal." Today, no other ideology has sufficient scope, allure, and trust to compete seriously with liberalism. Practically all countries of the world accept *de facto* and *de jure* the norms of Western civilization. There remain very few societies that ignore the norms of democracy, the market economy, and the free press, and those are in transition to the Western model. This is a sufficient reason to announce "the end of history," which if it has not arrived is about to. A similar conclusion was reached by neorealists, openly justifying US hegemony (Gilpin, Krauthammer), neoliberals (enthusiastically embracing the victory of democrats in the Eastern bloc), and certain postmodernists (seeing in globalization new horizons of human freedom).

Huntington opposes to this a "thick" analysis, which pays greater attention to the details, the qualitative aspects of the analysed processes, and he strives to better understand the deep dimension of the transformations of the post-bipolar world. He reaches the conclusion that modernization and democratization, and also the norms of market liberalism, in fact affected only Western societies, while all other countries accepted these rules of the game under the pressure of necessity, without including them in the depths of their cultures, pragmatically borrowing only separate applied and technological elements of Western civilization. Thus, Huntington speaks of the widespread phenomenon in non-Western countries of "modernization without Westernization," when representatives of non-Western societies borrow separate Western technologies, but strive to adapt them to local conditions and often direct them *against the West*. The democratization and modernization of non-Western countries thereby becomes, in light of a "thick" analysis, ambiguous and relative, and, hence, no longer guarantees the results that would be expected without taking into account the inner logic of these processes. The more the West expands its borders, including in them "the Rest, non-Western societies," the more this *ambiguity* is intensified, and the more the gap grows between the West and non-Western regions that have received new technologies and strengthened their potential, while preserving ties with traditional social structures. This circumstance leads to the concept of "civilization" as a technical IR concept.

Civilizations in the structure of 21st-century IR are broad spatial areas that, under the influence of modernization and relying on Western technology, strengthen their power and intellectual potential, but instead of fully accepting therewith the Western system of values preserve organic and strong ties with their own traditional cultures, religions, and social complexes, which sometimes sharply conflict with Western ones or even oppose them.

The collapse of the socialist camp only catalyzes these processes and lays bare this state of affairs. Instead of the symmetrical opposition East-West there emerges a field of tensions among several civilizations. These civilizations, today most often divided by national borders, will in the course of globalization and integration become more closely aware of their community and start to act in the system of international relations, guided by their own values and the interests proceeding from those values. As a result of the development of these processes and in the case of successful "modernization without Westernization," we will get a principally new picture of the balance of power on a world scale. This is the *multipolar world*.

Broadening the Spectrum of the Concept "Civilization" in the TMW: Definition

The concept "civilization" plays a key role in the Theory of a Multipolar World (TMW). Hence, it is extremely important to consider it in its different aspects and to give it various interpretations. In this question, it is premature to insist on a "strictly orthodox" or some other univocal definition, since we are dealing with a principally new theoretical context, corresponding to the ideational sphere in which it is alone possible to establish a full-fledged theory of multipolarity.

To become a juridical reality, "civilization" should be combined with what Schmitt called a "large space" and what in the TMW is regarded as a transitional theoretical model or "preconcept," located between this completed *de jure* formulation and the *de facto* existing civilizations. Thus, we can represent the current situation schematically:

1. Civilization (sociocultural fact);
2. Large space (geopolitical term, preconcept);
3. The legally formulated international order on the basis of the TMW (the legal side of the TMW).

In order to transition from the first level to the second, it is necessary to make more precise what is understood by "civilization." Here, a few approaches are possible. We will go through the main ones.

Civilization as Substance (the Ontological Concept of Civilization)

The examination of civilization of an autonomous substance proposes ascribing ontological priority to it. In this case, "civilization" corresponds to the Aristotelian category of "substance" and answers the question τὸ τί ἦν εἶναι.[1] This idea of civilization places it in the center of the conceptual field, which is expanded through predicates. If civilization corresponds to substance, then a collection of predicates describes it in each concrete case, predetermining its qualitative content. One civilization as substance is described by one set of predicates, another by another, etc.

Interactions and mutual influence between civilizations as substances can be traced. Substances as "things" (*res*) can be regarded as static and kinetic, and also as dynamic (from the point of view of their peculiar force-potential).

---

1 τὸ τί ἦν εἶναι is an Aristotelian term that is much debated because of its odd construction. The phrase literally means "the what-it-is being," often translated by scholars as essence or *being*.

Continuing the Aristotelian model, we can speak of the entelechies of civilizations and of the prospects of their gravitation toward their "natural places."

Civilization as Process (the Dynamic Concept of Civilization)

This approach proposes to consider civilizations in the framework of what Braudel called the "*la grande durée*," i.e. "cycles of long length." The first person to advance the theory of civilization as process was Norbert Elias (1939). In this case, a civilization is the constant change of all the elements, which becomes noticeable only when the civilization reaches its culmination point and enters into a period of revolutions, upheavals, or wars. But changes within the civilizational order always occur, although they most often remain unnoticeable to observers.

Thus, civilization is a condition in which on a microlevel constant fluctuations occur, changes accumulate, and relations among elements are transformed. Such an approach amounts to the method of the *Annales school* and differs significantly from the substantialist approach, based on the presumption of constant identity. The dynamic approach suggests, by contrast, that civilizational identity constantly changes, and, consequently, that each historical moment must be carefully examined and its semantic field necessarily studied in detail.

Civilization as System (the Systemic Concept of Civilization)

The systemic approach is on the whole close to the dynamic approach, but it puts at the center of attention changes of the general dominant, which expresses the totality of the balance of micro and meso processes. A civilization can be regarded in this case as a sociocultural system (Sorokin) or historico-cultural type (Danilevsky).

The systemic approach to civilization is also characteristic of Spengler (based on the dualism of civilization and culture), Toynbee (who proposed to extend the list of civilizations), and Gumilev (who combined the study of civilizations with the ethnological perspective and the original theory of "passionarity").

Civilization as Structure (the Structural-Functional/ Morphological Concept of Civilization)

In contrast to the systemic approach, the structural approach examines civilization as a constant phenomenon, whose changes within do not produce essential morphological change. The form of civilization remains constant in various phases of its existence and is expressed in the invariability of its basic structures.

It is another matter that these very structures and their "material" embodiment can change, and their expressions acquire a different character, manifesting through some or other ideological, religious, or cultural complexes. But at the same time the functional significance and correspondences among the main elements are in all cases preserved unchanged. In contrast to the substantialist approach, the structural approach emphasizes not ontological, but epistemological and gnoseological continuity.

Civilization as Paideuma (the Educational Concept of Civilization)

The theory of the *paideuma*, developed by representatives of the historic school of "cultural circles," and especially Leo Frobenius, can serve as a more precise version of the epistemological approach to civilization. Frobenius examines the transmission of cultures from one society to another as the transmission of a certain educational code, called a *paideuma*. The structure of this code predetermines the main civilizational practices, both in the domain of politics and economics and in the domain of spiritual culture, rituals, rites, symbols, etc.

Civilization, thus, is that in which one can and should be instructed.

The combination of the concept of civilization as *paideuma* with the model of "cultural circles" allows us to trace the path of diffusion of ancient civilizations and the continuation of this process in the contemporary world. In this model, the question of education occupies the center of attention.

Civilization as a Set of Values (the Axiological Concept of Civilization)

Civilization can be reduced to the totality of values that acquire the status of norms in some society. This axiological approach is contained in Weber's sociology and is well known. Without going into a detailed analysis of civilizational structures and without pretending to understand the logic of systemic development, the axiological approach allows one to describe a civilization operationally on the basis of its clearest signs (values), to build their systematic hierarchy, and to undertake comparative analysis.

This approach is convenient for express analysis and for the efficient composition of a "civilizational passport," in the spirit of what anthropologists (Geertz) call "thin description."

Civilization as Organized Unconscious (the Psychoanalytic Concept of Civilization)

The psychoanalyic interpretation of civilizations can be built on the later works of Freud himself (in particular, *Totem and Taboo*), where he proposes to apply the psychoanalytic to the analysis of cultural facts. In particular, in this reconstruction, the "Oedipus complex" is a socio-formative element for all human societies. Although this thesis was later contested by the representatives of social anthropology (who showed that in some cultures the preconditions for the "Oedipus complex" are lacking—in particular, in the matriarchal cultures of the aborigines of the Trobriand Islands), the idea of applying psycho-analysis to the interpretation of cultures proved its justifiability. Even more productive for the understanding of civilizations is Jung's idea of the "collective unconscious." Jung himself understood this differently in various phases of his work, but its different structure among representatives of various societies is an empirical fact. On this basis, one can build a psychoanalytic map of civilizations.

We can take as a special orientation the theory of Durand, who proposed his own version of the "sociology of depths," which allows for the interpretation of cultural and civilizational codes as results of the work of various modes of imagination.

Civilization as (Religious) Culture

The culturological interpretation of civilization is one of the most obvious approaches, all the more so since in some European languages civilization and culture are taken as synonymous terms. The specific character of this approach consists not only in emphasizing the cultural factor when defining a civilization and its qualitative content, but in heightened attention toward the religious bases of each concrete civilization, both when the religiosity is explicit and society-forming, and when it acts implicitly, through other, secular ideologies and value systems.

Civilization as Language (the Philological-Linguistic Conception of Civilization)

The definition of civilization as language proposes the examination of its structures from a linguistic and philological perspective. There are no strictly monolinguistic societies, nor *a fortiori* civilizations. Thus, in a civilization there is always one (sometimes two or more) *koiné* (lingua franca) and a full spectrum of other languages, inter-twined with the general semantic and conceptual bloc. Language and linguistic heritage can act as a general equivalent of civilization, which will allow for the comparison of civilizations with the help of the tools of comparative linguistics and semiotics.

At a certain level, this approach to civilization can be combined with a structuralist approach.

Civilization as the First Derivative from the Ethnos (the Ethnosociological Conception of Civilization)

In the book *Ethnosociology* a model is elaborated of the interpretation of societies and social structures through the method of relating them to the *ethnos* and its archaic condition. In this model, civilization is taken (alongside state and religion) as a technical term, signifying the transition from the *ethnos* to the *laos* (*narod*),[2] as a result of its first qualitative complexification. The *narod* differs from the *ethnos* in that its structure is more differentiated, it is socially stratified (elite and masses), the structures of Logos are imbued with strong positions, and the figure of the Other stands at the center of attention. In contrast to the state and religion, civilization embodies the high differential in culture, philosophy, and art. Often, state, religion, and civilization go hand in hand. Ethnosociology allows us to find the place of civilization as a historico-cultural phenomenon in the chain of other derivatives from the *ethnos*. In particular, it is apparent from this reconstruction that civilization relates to the paradigm of premodernity and to the forms of traditional society.

Civilization as Construct (the Constructivist Conception of Civilization)

An entirely different understanding of civilization can be had within the constructivist approach. This approach belongs to the para-digms of modernity and postmodernity. But if the primary object of constructed society in modernity is the state (the nation-state),

---

2 *laos* (λαός) is Greek for people.

civilization can be taken as a construct and result of projection under precisely postmodern circumstances. However, the liberal and in part Gauchist postmodernity more likely occupies itself with deconstructing all social structures, right up to their atomization and appeal to the singular individual (and then to Deleuze and Guatteri's rhizome, body without organs, and desiring machine). In the TMW and in the Fourth Political Theory, however, we encounter an alternative version of postmodernity, and in this context the object of construction can well become the civilization as a new, and in this case artificial, actor.

Civilization as Dasein (the Existential Conception of Civilization)

In the Fourth Political Theory (4PT), the subject is outlined through precisely the existential dimension and is identified with *Dasein*. The plurality of *Daseins* corresponds to the plurality of civilizations. This term was explicated in the book *Martin Heidegger: The Possibility of a Russian Philosophy*. Precisely this allows us to connect the 4PT and the TMW as two aspects of one and the same approach. Here, civilization can be described through a set of existentials, each of which will be characteristic of only one civilization. On this basis we can also trace the temporal horizons of civilization, described by Heidegger in *Being and Time*, applied, of course, to *Dasein*. The future of a civilization will thus consist in its possibility of being *authentically*. Consequently, each civilization will have its own concrete *Ereignis*.

Civilization as the Human's Normative Field (the Anthropological Conception of Civilization)

Finally, we can apply to civilization the method used by anthropologists to study illiterate cultures and archaic societies. Franz Boas showed that no measure can exist between societies and that comprehension of each of them demands inner participation, embedded observation, and even (temporary) change of identity. This theme was also developed by Boas's students, the American school of cultural anthropology, English representatives of social anthropology, the French sociological school of Durkheim and Mauss, structural anthropologists (Levi-Strauss), and German ethnosociologists (Thurnwald, Muhlmann).

From the very beginning, sociologists started to apply the anthropological approach to other, non-archaic societies (for instance, Thomas and Znaniecki in their classic work *The Polish Peasant in Europe and America*). Thus, all of the preconditions for the systematic study of civilizations with the help of anthropological tools are present and the paths of such an approach have already been approximately indicated.

Theoretically, it seems, we could identify other approaches to the study of civilizations, but here it is acceptable to stop their enumeration. Thirteen different, though not exclusive and more likely supplementary, approaches are enough to form an idea of the qualitative volume of possible civilizational studies. Each of these approaches can be combined with others and also directly with the domain of "large spaces." Geopolitics as a whole and the sociology of space allows us to carry out similar operations in the case of each concept of civilization. The spatial expression can have substance, process, system, structure, language, religion, culture, the unconscious, the *ethnos*, *Dasein*, and everything else. The totality of such maps, corresponding to various interpretations of civilization, will give the preconcept "large space" a huge semantic volume. From a preliminary approximation, "large space" will in each concrete case be transformed into a full-fledged and multidimensional semantic field. All this will prepare the last stage: transition to what Schmitt called the "order of large spaces," and in our case to a full-fledged legal formulation of a Multipolar World.

The Poles of a Multipolar World / List of Civilizations

Huntington identifies the following civilizations:

- Western civilization
- Orthodox (Eurasian) civilization
- Islamic civilization
- Hindu civilization
- Chinese (Confucian) civilization
- Japanese civilization (potential)
- Latin-American civilization
- Buddhist civilization
- African civilization

They are destined at a certain historic time to become the poles of a multipolar world.

Western Civilization

The most obvious civilization, often pretending to sole and universal status, is Western civilization. It begins in the Greco-Roman world and in the medieval era finally takes shape as the western half of the Christian Ecumene. Today, it consists of two strategic centers on either side of the Atlantic: North America (in the first place the US) and Western Europe. Modernity and its entire civilizational axiom system formed in this area. Here is located the indisputable and obvious pole of the present world order. Huntington calls this "the West." But in the picture of the plurality of civilizations, we see the following feature: the West as a civilization (*one of several!*) is a local phenomenon alongside other civilizations, with long histories and deep historical roots, which today possess serious resource, strategic, economic, political, and demographic potential. The West is a "large space" among other "large spaces." Western civilization leads, but *the rest*, if we combine their total potential, can at a certain moment throw down a challenge and call the hegemony of the West into question. Huntington himself naturally does not want this, but he realistically evaluates the situation, thinking that this will happen in any case, and so the leaders of Western civilization should already begin to take a very serious look at the troubled and risky future, where the likelihood of a clash with "the rest" will only grow with the extent of the growing power of other civilizations.

Orthodox (Eurasian) Civilization

Orthodox (Eurasian) civilization also has a Mediterranean origin, but it took shape on the basis of the Eastern Christian tradition, continuing the geopolitics of the Byzantine Empire. For more than a thousand years, the divergence between Western and Eastern Christianity has taken critical forms, and these two parts of the Christian Ecumene follow their own sometimes antagonistic historical paths. The core of Orthodox (Eurasian) civilization is Russia, which received, starting in the 15th century, a dual historical and geographical legacy: simultaneously from Ottoman-conquered Byzantium and from the collapsed Golden Horde, having become a synthesis of Eastern Christian and Steppe (Turanic) cultures.

The entire history of the relations of Russia and Western Europe is a conflict along a civilizational fault line, passing between Orthodox and Western Christianity (Catholicism and Protestantism). Later (in the reign of Peter) this opposition acquired the character of a conflict of national interests and even later (in the 20th century) was expressed in the conflict between global capitalism and global communism. And although this last version has passed, the civilizational identity of Russia and other Orthodox (in their history and culture) countries predetermines their essential difference from Western criteria, which easily spills over into a conflict of interests and under certain circumstances probable collision. Orthodox (Eurasian) civilization with its core in Russia has ever the basis for claiming the role of one of the poles of a multipolar world. In contemporary conditions, Russia hardly has enough potential to oppose the West alone, so a return to a bipolar system is impossible. But in the context of multipolarity, this civilization could well become a very important and in some cases *decisive* factor of the global balance of power. This has become particularly evident since 2000, when Moscow began to gradually reinforce its position in the international arena, overcoming the chaos of the 1990s.

Islamic Civilization

Islamic civilization is another *world power*. Today, Muslims are divided by the borders of nation-states, but there are points along which the representatives of Islamic civilization on the whole are in solidarity with one another, despite national borders. According to the extent of the modernization of Islamic societies and the fortification of their economic, political, military, and strategic potential, Islamic elites and intellectual circles recognize more and more distinctly the differences in the value systems between the Islamic world and Western civilization, which evokes constantly increasing anti-Western attitudes. The attack of the Islamic terrorist group Al Qaeda on the World Trade Center on September 11, 2001 shows how far this conflict can go. Along a number of parameters, Islamic civilization can full well claim the status of an independent pole of a multipolar world.

Chinese Civilization

The cultural pecularities of Chinese (Confucian) civilization are no less evident. Chinese society is united not so much by religion as by a common ethical culture, similarity of social attitudes, and many other ethical, spiritual, philosophical, and psychological features. The

Chinese are keenly aware of their civilizational peculiarity and are able to preserve fidelity to a cultural type, even when living among other, non-Chinese societies. Successfully assimilating Western technologies, the Chinese preserve their cultural identity almost untouched. Western individualism, hedonism, rationalism, etc. have not penetrated deep into Chinese society. Maintenance in the People's Republic of China of communist rule only underscores the uniqueness of the Chinese path. The impressive demography of the Chinese population represents an enormous political and economic resource, and the outstanding success of the Chinese economy has long since transformed China into a serious economic competitor of the countries of the West.

Hindu Civilization

India has no less demographic potential than China. It is obvious that India is not merely a state, but a civilization, with a many-thousand-year history, and specific philosophical and value attitudes that differ substantially from the norms of the contemporary West. The modernization of India is leading to certain changes in its social structure, but as technological development increases, so does the awareness of Hindus of their own civilizational identity. Hindu civilization is not aggressive, and contemplative in its roots, but also extremely conservative and steady, and it is able in the face of alternative civilizational codes (Islam, Westernization, etc.) to display a certain harshness. India's economic growth in the last few years also makes it a fully justified claimant to the role of a pole in a multipolar world. India has its strategies that it employs in a number of key areas of the subcontinent, on the borders with Pakistan, in a certain section of the Indian Ocean, and on the island states located there.

Japanese Civilization

Despite the fact that of all the non-Western countries Japan integrated into the zone of the "global West" the most deeply after the Second World War, Japanese civilization is a unique phenomenon with an independent cultural tradition. Japan's huge economic potential and the specific character of Japanese social psychology led many American analysts already at the start of the 1990s to think about a potential conflict of the West with Japan. In the last two decades, Japan's economic growth has noticeably slowed, and its political ambitions and regional policies, to say nothing of its global policies, have been significantly curtailed. Nevertheless, taking into account the past historical experience and the tremendous potential of Japanese society, it cannot be excluded that at a certain moment Japan will become alongside China one of the leading civilizational powers, at least in the Pacific region. It is already such, but, true, representing the strategic interests of the US, including in the question of balancing China's growing power. This "pro-Western" function of Japan might change in conditions of multipolarity.

Latin American Civilization

Latin American civilization is a post-colonial zone, politically organized by Europeans. But the historical ties with the Catholic and conservative cultures of Spain and Portugal, and also the significant percentage of an autochthonous population, became reasons for the culture of the countries of South America to differ substantially from the cultures of North America (where Anglo-Saxon Protestant influences prevailed and local Indian tribes were almost entirely destroyed). The religious, cultural, ethnosociological, and psychological differences of Latin Americans can serve as a precondition for the population of South America realizing its historical originality and becoming an independent pole, with its own agenda and strategic interests.

Various Latin American countries today are already moving in this direction, from the Venezuela of Hugo Chávez and the Bolivia of Evo Morales to Brazil, which has taken a powerful step forward in recent years. Together, the countries of Latin America possess significant demographic, resource, economic, and political potential and under certain circumstances could well become a pole of a multipolar world.

African Civilization

The remaining civilizations can be regarded as merely distant candidates for the status of poles in a multipolar world.

African civilization as a space subject to integration into an independent pole of a multipolar world exists in the form of a speculative project. The peoples of Trans-Saharan Africa are extremely isolated and united in nation-states along strictly colonial markers. They have no *shared* cultural identity or civilizational system. Theoretically, on the basis of racial, spatial, geopolitical, economic, and sociological peculiarities, the peoples of Africa could at some point recognize (more precisely, construct) their unity. Such projects exist; for instance, the United States of Africa (Kwame Nkrumah, Abdoulaye Wade, Muammar al-Gaddafi), the Organization of African Unity, the African Economic Community, etc. The aggregate of the population and territory makes this theoretical construction very impressive (third place in demography and first in territorial space worldwide). But in order for this zone to transform into an independent pole, a lot of time, it seems, must pass.

Buddhist Civilization

Buddhist civilization is also a foggy and imprecise notion. Different countries relate to it that differ in many cultural and social features from the neighbouring Islamic and Hindu civilizations. Buddhism is spread throughout China and Japan; however, these countries can claim to act as independent poles. Thus, the consolidation of Buddhist space, differing sharply from the area of Chinese or Japanese influence, can hardly come to pass in the near future. We can consider "Buddhist civilization" a reserve zone in the Pacific region.

The Map of a Potential Multipolar World

In this way, a simple enumeration of civilizations, both well formed and still approximate, allows us to impart a concrete character to the TMW. We get a differentiated structure of the potential map of a multipolar world. On this map, we see:

- *Western civilization*, today claiming universalism and hegemony, but in fact representing only one civilization among others, which means that its hegemony and universalism have strictly defined geographic borders and an entirely concrete historical context (and both the spatial and temporal borders can be moved in any direction, depending on the intercivilizational balance);

- *Orthodox (Eurasian) civilization*, whose approximate borders include the space of the CIS and part of Eastern and Southern Europe (this territory repeatedly acted in history as the main or at least a solid rival of Western civilization, right up to the recent dualism of East and West in the system of a bipolar world);

- *Islamic civilization*, a space encompassing North Africa, Central Asia, and a number of Pacific regional countries (containing huge demographic potential and a critically important volume of useful raw materials, including energy resources);

- *Chinese civilization*, including not only Taiwan, but also an extensive zone in the Pacific region, through which Chinese influence is spread (and which has certain reasons to become even more extensive, owing to Chinese demography and rate of economic growth);

- *Hindu civilization* (in which besides India we can place Nepal and Mauritius in Africa, where more than 50% of the population practice Hinduism);

- *Latin American civilization*, united by ties with the Spanish-Portuguese societies of Europe, the Catholic religion, a society of relatively mixed European-Indian-African culture (here we can include both the countries of South America and those of Central America, including Mexico at the northernmost point of this region);

- *Japanese civilization*, dwelling today in anabiosis, but historically having (justified, from the perspective of their power potential) claims to the establishment of a "Japanese order" throughout the Pacific region.

The contours of these civilizations are clearly discernable on the map and along a whole number of very important questions show *through* the borders of nation-states, which fragment the corresponding civilizational space.

The contours of three other potential civilizations are not as readily apparent. As integrated poles of a multipolar world, African and Buddhist civilizations represent today a distant reality.

Nevertheless, we are dealing with a ready outline of a world order, radically different from that which is the object of theorizations in the majority of IR paradigms, but positivist and classic, on one hand, and postpositivist, on the other. This map of civilizational centers in a system of multipolarity is a *diagram of a possible and even likely future*. In this future, the number of actors of world politics will be strictly greater than one or two, but less than the number of currently existing nation-states.

Each civilization will be a pole of power and a center of local hegemony, surpassing the potential of all the elements (relating to a given civilization), but lacking sufficient might to impose its will on neighbouring civilizations.

The multipolar order will thus reproduce the Westphalian system on another level: with its sovereignty, balance of powers, chaos of the international sphere, possibilities of conflict and potential world negotiations, but only with the principal difference that the actors will henceforth be *not nation-states*, normatively imagined along a single model, copied from the European capitalist states of modernity, but *civilizations*, with an entirely independent internal structure, corresponding to historical traditions and cultural codes.

Such a world will be *polycentric* in the full sense of the word, since the equality of civilizations on the level of the international order will not imply the identity of their domestic arrangements. Each civilization will thus get the right to organize its societies in accordance with its own preferences, value systems, and historical experiences. In some, religion will play the decisive role; in others, secular principles might well prevail. Some might have democracy; others, entirely different political forms of rule, either connected with historical experience and cultural particularities, or chosen by the societies themselves as rival projects. In contrast to the Westphalian system, in this model of world order there will be no planetary model of universalist hegemony, no pattern obligatory for all. In each civilization it will be possible to assert a general system of values characteristic only of the given civilization, including notions of the subject, object, time, space, politics, the human, consciousness, the goal and meaning of history, rights and duties, social norms, etc. Each civilization has its own philosophy, and non-Western systems, naturally, will rely on their own indigenous philosophical systems, reviving them, perfecting them, transforming them or even exchanging them for new ones, but all of this within the context of the exclusive freedom and support of a concrete society.

Civilizations as Constructions

Here we come to a very important point. Many of Huntington's critics advanced counter-arguments, disputing the very existence of civilizations in the contemporary world, or indicating that after a certain period, globalization, Westernization, and modernization even out cultural and civilizational differences. They thus raise the question of the ontology of the concept of civilization with full acuity.

The fact that civilizations exist as a cultural and moral background (sometimes religious) that unites broad segments of societies is an empirical, sociological and historical fact. But is this enough under present circumstances for this unity to be sufficiently well recognized, mobilized, and turned into a strong political idea, capable of making civilizations the main actors in a system of international relations?

Huntington adduces empirical observations, insisting that such an ontology does exist and that under present circumstances precisely civilizational identity is called on to play a decisive role in the unfolding of the main processes, given the end of the bipolar world, the growing difficulties of the US in coping with the spread of its borders in the unipolar moment, and the background of globalization, which, together with the universalization of certain codes and procedures, facilitates the revival of local and religious identities (Robertson and his "glocalization"). But this is debatable. Supporters of a civilizational approach insist that civilization is an ontologically justified concept in the sphere of international relations; opponents insist that this ontology is doubtful and not real. Since Huntington himself stands on the side of the West and is an integral part of its intellectual elite, his conception of the civilizational factor goes with the positions of the West, and Huntington sees only a threat in the very fact of the existence of civilizations other than the West, and all the more so in their likely strengthening and becoming independent poles of a multipolar world. He considers this threat real and ontologically grounded. That is why he is regarded as a pessimist of globalization. At the same time,

for him the ontology of the concept of civilization is the estimation of
the seriousness and reality of the potential adversary.

However, we can approach this question from an entirely different perspective, but within the framework of a realist approach, to
which Huntington himself remains faithful in many questions, but
on the basis of the constructivist method and, more broadly, of postpositivist IR theories. For the TMW it is not that important whether
civilizations exist as actors and poles of the multipolar world, whether
their existence is a demonstrated and weighty factor or a weak and
turbulent hindrance on the path of the certain onset of unipolarity
or West-centric globalization. Civilizations as actors of international
relations is not at all a return to pre-modernity, where traditional
states and empires figured. Civilizations as actors of international relations is something *entirely new*, something that has never been before,
a kind of *reality of postmodernity*, called on to take the place of the
exhausted potential of the world order based on the dominance of the
Westphalian system, a *postmodern alternative to* both the unipolar
American empire and non-polar globalization. In other words, in
some sense a civilization can be regarded *as a construct*, as a specific
discourse, as a text, which, however, has a structure differing principally from the homogeneous, "monotone" West-centric discourse.
Civilization is the infusion into the reality of international relations
of qualitative difference (*Différance*), where humanity is thought of
not as the reproduction of a homogeneous series (the presumption of
civil rights or the ideology of human rights), but as a set of independent monads (according to Leibniz), which organize several parallel
semantic and cultural universes. These universes come into *conflict*
(as in Huntington), but it is not at all necessary that they come *only*
into conflict. Just as likely is a *dialogue of civilizations*, on which the
former President of Iran Khatami insisted. There can be *any* form of
interaction of civilizations as actors of a multipolar world: confrontational or peaceful; in practically the same proportions as relations
are established among nation-states in the Westphalian system. But if

nation-states and national sovereignty were constructs of modernity, civilizations can full well become a *construct of postmodernity*, expressing thereby a *radical plurality of discourses that cannot be reduced to a common denominator*.

The Coordinating Center of Multipolarity

Civilizations are that which needs to be created. However, this process of creating civilizations does not wholly presuppose an artificial model, completely absent in reality. There is a cultural, sociological, historical, mental, psychological base for civilizations, and it is empirical. But the transition from civilization as a cultural and sociological given to civilization as an actor of the multipolar world requires *effort*. It is a task that a certain historical authority can and must carry out.

What is this authority? We can define it conditionally and approximately as the *political and intellectual ideological elite of "the Rest,"* i.e. the aggregate of state actors, intellectuals, representatives of big monopolies and religious structures, and also the leading political powers of those countries, which for some reason or other do not agree with unipolarity or West-centric globalization, support "modernization without Westernization," and see the future of their societies only in the framework of a world order that differs from the current one.

Huntington himself, following Toynbee, speaks of the pair "the West and the Rest" as civilizational antagonists. Gradually, "the Rest" will acquire mature features and settle its historic program in the elaboration of a TMW.

Precisely the intellectual elite of the non-Western world is called on to *construct multipolarity* and, accordingly, to transform "civilization" into an effectual and substantial concept.

The Borders of Civilizations

One very important question is how to determine the *borders of civilizations* and hence also the likely models of relations among civilizations. Here we can consider different variations, but several points are immediately obvious. The borders of civilizations cannot be and are not fixed by *lines*, as in the case of the borders that divide nation-states. Civilizations are separated from one another in space by *broad zones*, in which a mixed civilizational identity is present. Moreover, within a civilization there can be fairly big enclaves or inclusions of another civilization. A civilization relates to space radically differently than a nation-state to its territory. The extent of administrative regulation correlates not so much with space as with societies, communities, and population groups. Thus, the territorial feature is here not as unambiguous as in the case of belonging to one or another national territory.

Accordingly, borders between nations should have a *qualitatively different status* than borders between states. On the borders between civilizations there can be entire autonomous worlds, independent and isolated, comprised of absolutely unique social structures and cultural ensembles. A separate legal model should be devised for them that takes into account the peculiarities of overlapping civilizations, the proportions between them, and also their qualitative content and the level of intensity of the recognition of their identity. Some schools of jurisprudence distinguish the concepts "border" (in the strict sense, as a line separating the territory of one country from another) and "frontier" (as a less concrete area, between one type of space and another). In the first case, it is precisely a line, without width; in the other, it is an area, a zone, something with width. In this context, one civilization is separated from another by precisely a "frontier," an intercivilizational zone, which can be rather broad and diffuse, specific in each case, and different from the sociocultural space on either side of the "frontier."

The Practice of a Multipolar World: Integration

Now that we have clarified the ontological status of the concept of "civilization," the direction of the main vector of practice in the construction of a multipolar world becomes clear. We are speaking of *integration.*

Integration becomes the axis of the multipolar world order. But in the TMW this integration should take place within a strictly civilizational framework. Thus, we should distinguish several types of integration:

- *global*, which does not take account of civilizational peculiarities and proceeds on the basis of a universal protocol, founded on the Western system of norms, procedures, and values;

- *hegemonic*, which leads to the establishment of hierarchical, disproportionate relations among the subjects of integration, without taking account of cultural differences;

- *civilizational*, which embraces only those countries and societies with a shared cultural constitution and similar sociopolitical system, as well as shared historical (and religious) roots.

The TMW insists on opposing the first two types of integration and encouraging and actively conducting the third type of integration. Thus, we get a concrete group of several integrational zones, rather distinct in their civilizational content:

- *Western integration* (European and American), and also Euro-Atlantic (here everything is successful; there is the military-political NATO bloc, the European Union, projects of integrating the entire North American continent, including a North American currency, the "amero");

- *Eurasian integration* (its reference point is the Eurasian Union, and its stages are intensification of military-strategic cooperation within the CSTO, economic partnership within the framework of the EurAsEC, the union state of Russia-Belarus, the project of a Unified Economic Space, taking into account Ukraine in particular, the CIS);

- *Islamic integration* (the Islamic Conference, the Islamic Bank of Development, the sole Shiite space from Iran and Iraq to Libya, and also the fundamentalist project of a "new Caliphate");

- *Chinese integration* (ASEAN+China, Taiwan's likely absorption by China, introducing the zone of a "golden yuan");

- *Hindu integration* (strengthening Hindu influence in South-East Asia, on the Indian subcontinent, in Nepal, in numerous Pacific basin countries that are close to India geopolitically and culturally);

- *Japanese integration* (currently under question and including the growth of Japan in the Far East);

- *Latin American integration* (Latin American Association integration, Mercosur, the Central American common market, etc.);

- *African integration* (Organization of African Unity, United States of Africa, etc.).

Integration becomes the priority process in the organization of a multipolar order in international relations.

The Preconcept: Civilization and the "Large Space"

In the course of building a multipolar world, at a certain point the question will arise in full force of the translation of the concept of "civilization" from a sociocultural category into a *legal concept*. Extremely important here is the concept of a "large space" (*Großraum*), developed by the German philosopher and jurist Carl Schmitt. The significance of Schmitt's idea for the sphere of IR was compellingly shown by the English IR theorist Fabio Pettito. Schmitt raised the question of how international norms are formed that in time acquire a generally accepted legal status. He was especially interested in the establishment of such a phenomenon as the *Jus Publicum Europeum*, which laid the foundations for the European system of IR in modernity. On the whole Schmitt follows a realist position, so for him the primary question is the question of *procedure* of correlating the sovereign nation-state (over which there is by definition no higher authority) and the elaboration of rules in the sphere of international relations, to which, nevertheless, nation-states must submit. Usually the presence of an institutional ordering of anarchy in international relations is admitted by precisely liberals, which is why in some classifications they are called "institutionalists." In the case of Schmitt, we are dealing with a convinced realist who nevertheless gave fixed attention to the structured environment of international relations. Hence, the paradoxical character of his approach: "institutional realism."

As the basic preconditions of realism in IR, chaos and anarchy in international relations are regulated, according to Schmitt, not simply by appeal to shared liberal-democratic values, trade competition, and pacifism, but specifically by a perceived balance of power, correlated with the concrete geographic situation. Having given a lot of attention to geopolitics, Schmitt insists on the fixation of legal norms in a geographic space. As a result, the entire sphere of IR proves to be correlated with a physical and political map. Chaos in IR thus acquires spatial features and is structured by the force-lines of the balance of power of various states.

Since the Westphalian system formally rejects the acknowledgement of any legitimate and legal reality above national sovereignty, the spatial normativization of the sphere of international relations does not and cannot receive formally conceptualized expression. Nevertheless, the balance of power is often so steady and obvious that it can essentially be compared to a law and, as a result, be fixed in law. This was the fate of the "Monroe Doctrine" or the conditions of the Westphalian world: the dominant world powers identified their national interests (confirmed by their power resources) with the normative state of affairs, even when at issue were processes taking place not only beyond their immediate borders, but at a great distance from them. Schmitt analyzed in detail the process of this delicate work, which led in the last phase to the emergence of supranational legal structures, having a different degree of obligatoriness from and to a certain extent conceptually conflicting with the generally accepted Westphalian system of national sovereignty. For this analysis, Schmitt introduces the term "preconcept" as a kind of *political idea* having a supranational scale and not yet fixed in legal codes, but capable under certain circumstances and a concrete balance of powers of acquiring legal status.

Next, Schmitt relates the "preconcept" (for instance, the "Monroe Doctrine" or "German Reich") to the spatial borders to which the preconcept can be applied. As a result, a new form arises, the *"large space"* (*Großraum*), which is one of the most important elements of Schmitt's political theory. A *"large space"* is the spatial expression of a legal preconcept in the domain of IR.

If we apply this procedure to our concept of "civilization," we will find that it applies ideally to the TMW. Multipolarity, as, incidentally, also bipolarity or unipolarity, is not a legal concept and cannot become one in the near future or perhaps at all. It is a description of the factual balance of power among leading world actors. Consequently, both *"civilization"* and *"multipolar order"* have the status of legal preconcepts: they exist, they can by force or with resources be corroborated, they can be declared, they can be effectual and real. Under certain circumstances, they can even replace the Westphalian model, and then it will be natural to raise the question of the formal rejection of national sovereignty, transferring the concept of sovereignty to a different authority, to *civilization* or the poles of a multipolar world. In this case, the preconcept will become simply a concept and legal notion. But events can unfold according to a different logic: in this case, civilization and multipolarity will remain preconcepts for a certain long period of time (like the way bipolarity did not abolish national sovereignty, though it made it relative for all those countries that did not have the status of a superpower).

When we try to draw the borders of civilizations, we will directly encounter the "large space," a concept that is very convenient because of its preconceptual status for fixing the spatial localization of civilizations.

The multipolar world, based on the balance of power of its component civilizations, can be called, following Schmitt, *"the order of large spaces."*

Politeia in the Theory of a Multipolar World

Civilizations are the actors of international relations in the TMW. We saw that the understanding of civilization can be extremely diverse; at the same time, different versions do not exclude but supplement each other. This variety significantly enriches the concept, makes it extremely substantial, which gives rise to the possibility of plural interpretations of civilizational identity, whose proportions, emphases, and borders can change, become more precise, and vary. But to move to the level of theory, this conceptual pluralism should be reduced to a simpler system. Here, the most important instrumental concept is "large space" (*Großraum*), considered in the "Geopolitics of a Multipolar World." A "large space," in contrast to a civilization, which is fundamentally not a political phenomenon, can be regarded as a political preconcept, leading closely to the formulation of the political dimension of the TMW. Here we come to a very important problem: what political status will the poles of a multipolar world (civilizations) have in this theory? And accordingly, on what basis will the legal foundation of international relations be built?

Here we must answer directly a very delicate question, having both purely theoretical and psychological significance: will the poles of the multipolar world be *states*? If yes, of what kind? If not, then what will they be?

In order to answer these questions and approach the elaboration of a formal political concept, concluding the construction of a TMW (at least in its first phase), we have to give a brief overview of what is understood by "state" in contemporary political science. On a historical scale, it is customary to divide the state into two types: the premodern state and the modern state. These are fundamentally different concepts, each with a unique set of attributes. The premodern state reaches its general culmination in Empire, which proposes the combination of the highest central authority in a single center with the broad distribution of power to political formations of a lower level: provinces, colonies, semi-autonomous kingdoms, etc. Another type of premodern state is the ancient *polis*, the city-state, a small, autonomous unit, with relative independence from other analogous units, that serves as the center of authority for nearby (rural) territories. Premodern states can vary greatly in terms of political authority, which Aristotle systematized into three pairs, the first member of which is considered a positive version of rule, and the second as negative, corrupted, pejorative: monarchy-tyranny, aristocracy-oligarchy, politeia-democracy. Large territories prefer more centralization (monarchy), while small territories can be run in the regime of direct rule by the people [*narodopravlenie*] (*politeia*). That is, we relate Empire or the city-state as versions of the premodern state to premodernity not on the basis of their political system. This is important. The main criteria distinguishing the premodern from the modern state are the following:

- the presence in premodern states of a suprarational mission and mythical origins;

- the presence at their basis of the distribution of the powers of an estate society;

- the presence of collective identity (caste, estate, ethnic, confessional, etc.) as the social basis of the political organism.

The modern state differs from the traditional state in precisely these three points. It:

- is completely rational, led by calculation and national interests, and created on the basis of a social contract;
- proposes the equality of all citizens before the law and the absence of strictly defined privileges to rule for any social group;
- is based on individual citizenship, i.e. it denies on a legal level any form of collective identity.

The modern state is usually called a "nation-state" or "state-nation" (*État-Nation*).

Today in international relations only the "nation-state" is the norm, which is considered the sole legitimate pattern.

In political science, there are heated debates about the nature and structure of the modern nation-state, but the basis for most scholars remains the analysis of the state by Weber and his contemporary followers, sometimes called "neo-Weberians" (Mann, Skocpol, Tilly, etc.).

The Weberian tradition defines the state along four basic elements. The state is:

- a *differentiated* set of institutions and personnel, embodying
- *centralism*, in the sense that political relations are organized as radiating outward from within, covering
- the entire *territorially fixed zone*, over which
- it possesses *a monopoly on the establishment of rules of domination*, supported by a monopoly on the use of the means of physical violence.

This Weberian model of the sociology of the state describes it precisely from the perspective of form and presupposes to a certain
extent its autonomy (a doctrine of absolute sovereignty underlies this
model as its implicit axiom). Marxists introduce into this picture an
additional social aspect, insisting that class relations play a major role,
tending toward transcending national borders (the class solidarity of
the international bourgeoisie and the international character of the
proletariat). But even if one does not acknowledge the idea of a class
struggle, Marxist analysis gives heightened attention to the social
side, to civil society, which does not have a direct relation to the state
as a political form, but nevertheless exerts a significant (sometimes
decisive) role on politics. This was worked out in detail by Gramsci
and contemporary Gramscians (both left and right). Gramsci located
"civil society" in the superstructure and strictly distinguished it from
the sphere of the political (the state). If in politics (the state) we are
dealing with direct power, legally formulated and acknowledged functionally (Schmitt's *Potestas Directa*), in society we are dealing with
what Gramsci called "hegemony," i.e. with a form of establishment
of hierarchical and power relations that is not recognized as such by
those on whom it is imposed. We can relate hegemony in Gramsci's
understanding with Schmitt's *Potestas Indirecta*. Hegemony is not recognized as power by those over whom it acts. It is not acknowledged
legally and does not have any legal status. The communist Gramsci
thinks that in bourgeois society the bourgeoisie has not only political power with the help of the bourgeois state and its apparatus, but
also hegemony, expressed in education, pedagogy, science, culture,
philosophy, art, and other forms of civil society, where the carriers
of bourgeois consciousness implicitly dominate, consolidating and
legitimating the intellectual, political dominance of the capitalists.
The significance of the factor of "hegemony" in the Gramscian understanding substantially supplements the Weberian definition of
the state with an additional social dimension. The significance of the
role of civil society and other variants of *Potestas Indirecta* is willingly

acknowledged and even ideologically employed by many liberals, transnationalists, and even the "New Right" (Benoist).

Finally, another important conceptual move in understanding the nature of the state is made by the neorealists in IR (Waltz, in the first place), which propose to examine the structure of the nation-state not "outward from within," like classical Weberian analysis, but "inward from without," analyzing how the general balance of power in world politics affects not only the foreign policies of separate states, but partly their domestic policies, forcing nation-states to adapt — politically, economically, socially, culturally, etc. — to the political system that has formed on an international level. Representatives of the neo-Weberian approach develop this same theme, adding geopolitical factors and the "balance of power" analysis of the state itself.

The English School of international relations is a synthesis of such an approach, especially the stream associated with Halliday, called "historical sociology in IR." In the representatives of this approach, we encounter all three levels in the understanding of the state: the Weberian (formal), the sociological (both Gramscian and liberal/ transnational), and the geopolitical (taking into account the global system of the balance of power).

This brief overview of the conception of the modern state helps us approach an answer to the earlier question: is it possible to examine the pole of a multipolar world, the civilization, as the basic actor in the syntax of state?

Now we can try to take an inductive path and grope for the characteristics that must be characteristic of the poles of a multipolar world. We will try to describe them intuitively:

- *A pole of the multipolar world should be sovereign.* But only in the face of other poles. This follows from the practical demand of ensuring the civilization's freedom and independence before other civilizations, based on alternative cultural codes;

- *the center of power in a civilization should be legal,* from a formally legal perspective;

- the area of the application of power and, accordingly, the domain of its establishment of the rules of the game should be *differentiated,* depending on the ethnocultural and confessional composition of the population;

- the territorial model of rule is built on principles of *federalism* and *subsidiarity* (Althusser);

- the identity of units integrated into the civilization can be *variant* — collective (primarily) and individual (in some cases);

- the political formation should have both a *mission* (proceeding from the civilization's cultural code) and *rational interests* (based on verified and obvious calculations);

- *social strata* (ethnoconfessional groups, etc.) should be transparently and legally represented in the structure of the political body;

- it is necessary for there to be an *intercivilizational council* as an advisory organ, establishing (not absolutely and not invariably) the rules of intercivilizational interaction (without upsetting the principle of the sovereignty of civilizations) and taking into account both the principle of multipolarity and the balance of powers.

Now, if we analyze this set of intuitive parameters, we find, to our surprise, that such a theoretically constructed political body, on one hand, operates with known, and theoretically justified in other contexts, qualities of the Political and, on the other, does not coincide with any other model, not with the premodern state, nor with the modern state, nor with the transnational constructs of neoliberals, nor with Marxist international projects. We are dealing with centralism in the conception of power, sovereignty, and legality, but at the same time with pluralism in regard to social identity and territorial right, and, moreover, with a high level of legalization of what Gramsci called "civil society." Thus, we obtained an original concept, which cannot be strictly identified with the state (with empire of the nation-state), with society, or with any other usual model of the Political, although all its elements, taken separately, prove familiar.

In a certain sense, we are dealing with the description of one version of the Political of postmodernity.

It remains to select a name for this conception. We propose (as an option) to use the term *politeia* in the Platonic sense (not in the narrow sense of "positive democracy," as Aristotle used it in the *Politics*). The Platonic *Politeia* (a famous dialogue, in which the teaching of ideas is coherently and systematically presented) is translated both as "State" [in Russian] and as "Republic." Nevertheless, the reality at issue in Plato's work and the meaning the Greeks gave to the word at the time do not coincide with today's conceptions of the state or with what the Romans understood by *Res Publica* (nor, all the more so, what we mean by republic today). A *politeia* is a political formation *of any dimension*: from a full-fledged centralized state to its separate parts (provinces, regions, satraps, and even very small village units or confessional enclaves). This term is sometimes used in political science, but most often metaphorically, without any strictly fixed conceptual denotation. What impedes us in this case from fixing as such a denotation the set of qualities possessed by a pole in the multipolar world? The more so, since the term *politeia* does not have a fixed meaning in the political theories of either modernity or premodernity. A *politeia* is an ordered, organized society, which an empire, a modern state, its separate parts, and also societies of various calibres can be, from small communities to global society. Theoretically, we can apply the term *politeia* to all of them, which is not used precisely because of its tremendous polysemy. But the same polysemy that explains why this term did not receive broad application in political science is in the case of the theory of a multipolar world a wonderful terminological advantage, full well corresponding to the very structure of multipolarity as a complex phenomenon. *Politeia* is a concept ideally suited for describing *the complex Political*, the reduction of which to a concept demands the inclusion of a greater number of parameters of diverse dimension than are at work in the routine practice of modernity. A state is a *politeia*, but a *politeia* is not the state, since it includes also society, culture, and even geopolitical units. The *politeia* is in the TMW the political form of the "large space" and hence possesses from the start also a geopolitical dimension, which allows us to transparently integrate the "geopolitics of multipolarity" into the TMW.

If we set the term *politeia* for the pole of a multipolar world, we will see another linguistic parallel: in interpreting the meaning of the Greek word *politeia*, dictionaries often suggest as the closest concept in meaning the Latin term *civitas*, which gives us precisely the civilization. But we saw precisely the civilization as the main actor of international relations in the TMW. That is, the search for a political concept to describe the pole of a multipolar world ended precisely where we began: we came again to the notion of "civilization," but this time specifying its political expression and content.

Theory of a Multipolar World and Other Paradigms of IR

The Relevance of Realism to the TMW

AFTER THEIR ORIGINALITY and difference from existing approaches in IR have been distinctly specified and clarified, civilization as the basic actor in IR and the TMW built on this basis can, on a new level, be related to existing theories, but now not as derivatives, but as a new *independent paradigm* with other, already existing paradigms. This juxtaposition will help us outline more fully the specific character of the TMW and its structure and will help us study an even more important point: the clarification of how relations between civilizations can form in theory and whether conflict (as Huntington thought) or dialogue (as Khatami or Pettito thought) will prevail.

Realism is for the actors of civilizations. The realist paradigm, operating with the norms of the Westphalian system and advancing as an actor nation-states, is straightforwardly entirely inapplicable to the TMW. The difference in actors presupposes an entirely different understanding of the milieu of international relations. If we apply the realist paradigm literally, we will see that instead of a map of civilizations and "large spaces" we will have a political map of the world, where civilizational zones are divided (often artificially) into a series of nation-states, while some states are the intersection of two or more civilizations. Realists insist that "the state is a wolf to states," or, in the extreme case, they recognize the hierarchical relations of hegemony. But such an approach blocks any attempt to integrate "large spaces" on a civilizational basis. Consequently, in its pure form, realism is unacceptable and inapplicable. Supporters of the TMW find themselves in this case in polemics against the representatives of classical realism and neorealism.

But if we take civilizations as the main actors of international relations, fixed in "large spaces," we get an entirely different picture. In this case, we can imagine *intercivilizational* relations as a direct analogue to the structure of the international sphere in the realist paradigm. Here we should also postulate chaos and anarchy, but on a new level: as *intercivilizational* chaos and *intercivilizational* anarchy.

Repeating the logic of the realists, we can say that there is no supracivilizational level in the TMW and no universal scale of values that could act as a generally accepted norm in relations among civilizations. The civilizational, multipolar approach presumes the complete uniquness of each civilization, and it is not possible to find a common denominator for them all. This is the essence of multipolarity as *pluriverse*. Each civilization itself formulates and presents its concept of man, society, norm, truth, knowledge, being, time, space, God, world, history, politics, etc. So, dialogue between civilizations is possible to the same extent as conflict, but impossible is the transition from several civilizations to a single one. Consequently, on this level the TMW can fully borrow the logic of traditional realists, rejecting the ontology and stability of international institutions and norms, but apply it to an entirely different environment, not international (inter-state), but intercivilizational. *Changing the subject of the world order means changing its [i.e. the order's] qualitative content.* If realists think that all states strive to optimize their interests and rationalize the means and mechanisms of their accomplishment, in the case of civilizations this reductionist schema does not work. Civilizations can have entirely different goals and motivations. Some are inclined to expand; others, to maximalize their material power; others, to technological development; others, to contemplation; others, to preserve themselves in isolation; others, to active dialogue with the surrounding world and the exchange of cultural forms. Here, a "thin" approach to IR is not at all suitable, since the civilization as subject is so multidimensional and unique, original and peculiar, that a "thick" approach becomes not simply desirable, but necessary and obligatory.

Modelling the profile of a civilization is a unique task every time, and clarifying general features can only happen *a posteriori*, not *a priori*. This is a second limitation of realism. If realists understand the principles of "self-help" and national interests as a general rule of parameters characteristic of practically all nation-states, the TMW insists that among civilizations the list of basic parameters is much *broader* and *voluminous*, and also more diverse. Thus, both chaos and anarchy in the intercivilizational sphere acquire a more complex structure: it is not simply a field of struggle of approximately identical actors with different power potentials and a similar system of interests and aims, but a multidimensional and multilayered labyrinth, where *nonlinear* regularities, strange attractors, and the phenomenon of turbulence are at work. The composition of the map of intercivilizational anarchy is a much more complicated matter than the analysis of anarchy in classical realism, and even in neorealism.

But with these two fundamental corrections, many logical aspects of realism can be successfully set in motion in the elaboration of a TMW.

In particular, the most important borrowing from classical realism can be the critique of the possibility of supracivilizational institutions. Neorealism, with its inclination to build a structural system based on the balance of power, can full well be applied to a multipolar world order, which in its basic parameters will also be organized in accordance with the power potential of the main actors (only, they will be civilizations in the given case). In a certain sense, civilizations as poles of a multipolar world will be regional *hegemonies*, with all the consequences that follow from this. At the same time, there must be more than three such hegemonies.

Neorealist constructions, which study precisely hegemonic models as a priority, can be very useful in building a TMW. And Waltz's theory about the stability of a bipolar model, which is now on the periphery, refuted by the facts of the 80s and 90s, can be introduced anew in the constitution of a multipolar model, put in place of a bipolar one.

The Relevance of Liberalism to the TMW

The TMW can borrow separate aspects from the liberal paradigm, too. Liberalism insists that similar political regimes (although they only speak of liberal democracies) are inclined to integrate and to consolidate multilayered sociocultural, economic, and network ties, with the prospect of also shared supranational institutions. The culture of political democracy creates the conditions for overcoming national egoism. If we cast off the universalism typical for the West of the practically "ethnocentric" appeal to "democracy," we get the thesis: societies *with similar cultures* are inclined to integration and the creation of supranational structures. If we apply this to the zone of shared civilization, we will find ourselves on the wave of the TMW. Indeed, integrational processes and the creation of suprastate structures on the basis of a shared sociocultural matrix occur *more easily* than in other cases. In the context of a civilization, it is not so much the political regime of the state (democracy) as *culture (and often religion) that matters*. Thus, relations between states with a common culture (religion) are built according to a completely different logic than relations between states with different cultures.

A commonality of culture is for the TWM a necessary condition for successful integration into a shared "large space" and, accordingly, for the creation of a pole of a multipolar world. The significance of the cultural factor as not less important than the principle of sovereignty brings the supporters of the TMW closer to liberals than to classical realists, who insist on the sovereignty of precisely nation-states without taking into account the cultural factor. (Schmitt and other "institutional realists" are an exception, in particular several representatives of the English School of IR). But this proximity is actual only when emphasis on the "political regime" (democracy) is replaced by emphasis on belonging to a common culture (religion).

The liberal paradigm, and especially neoliberalism and transnationalism, pay much attention to processes of globalization. In practice, globalization has a few stages. First, regional integration occurs, then universal, planetary integration. But for liberals in IR, regional globalization is only a transitional condition and preliminary phase of worldwide globalization, lacking any particular value and only preparing the way for the sought after outcome, the onset of a "global world" and the "end of history."

The TMW, for its part, supports regional globalization and integration for the reason that these processes in practice always occur in the borders of some concrete civilization. Arguments among the countries of the European Union about accepting Turkey into this supranational structure clearly show that even among Europeans who ignore all religio-cultural aspects of the identity of society the sensation of the foreignness of Turks provokes serious apprehension.

But if for liberals and globalists this is a temporary difficulty, supporters of the TMW, by contrast, *conceptualize precisely regional integration*, which they regard as an independent and finished process, whole in itself, and moreover do not propose any other integrational phases after it. In accordance with the spirit of multipolarity, regional integration is thought of not as a step or phase of planetary globalization, but as an autonomous historico-political, strategic, and social process, having its end in itself. Integration must *end* with the attainment of the civilization's natural borders. After this, the phase begins of specifying the proportions and systems of influence in the zone of the "frontier."

Regional globalization brings supporters of the TMW closer to liberals in IR, while their attitude toward planetary globalization, by contrast, divides them.

But if we accept these two fundamental corrections (cultural unity instead of the unity of political regimes and regional globalization instead of planetary globalization), supporters of the TMW can full well borrow arguments from representatives of the liberal theory of IR, especially when it is necessary to refute the theories of realists strictly holding to a state-centric approach. Moreover, liberals developed a number of themes that are also relevant for the TMW.

In the first place, this is the *idea of peace or a zone of peace*, which is a priority center of attention for IR liberals. If we look at history, we will notice that the concept "peace" has everywhere been connected with a necessary specification: which peace exactly? We know *Pax Romana, Pax Turcica, Pax Britannica, Pax Russica*, and, finally, the contemporary *Pax Americana*. This word usage of the term "peace" with an addition that specifies whose peace it is, who is responsible for it and for the preservation of order, is very revealing. If we relate this addition to civilizations, we will get a *multipolar theory of peace* (in the sense of *Pax*, peace), consisting of several zones where peace will reign, based each time on concrete civilizational principles. We get: Pax Atlantica (consisting of Pax Americana and Pax Europaea), Pax Eurasiatica, Pax Islamica, Pax Sinica, Pax Hindica, Pax Nipponica, Pax Latina, and later Pax Buddhistica, Pax Africana. These zones of civilizational peace (as the absence of war) and general security can be taken as the basic concepts of multipolar pacifism. The task of civilizations as actors of international relations is in the first place to make them zones of stable peace, since in the opposite case they will not be able to act in a consolidated manner at a global level. At the same time, multipolar peace (*Pax Multipolaris*) should have its own ontology in the context of international relations: it assumes simultaneously

a supranational, suprastate level (which is why there is international
and foreign peace with regard to the state), but not "universal" and
not "planetary" (i.e. internal, with regard to civilizations).

The second important point for the TMW consists in the neoliberal concept of interdependence and expansion of the list of actors.
Here we should also move everything liberals say about all humanity
to the level of civilization. Civilization assumes the presence of a sociocultural, geopolitical, and economic zone, where there are closely
intertwined structures and communities relating to this civilization,
and to a much greater extent than under conditions of division by
national borders. In the TMW, civilizational networks replace global
networks, but their functions remain very similar in other respects. In
a civilization, various levels of sociopolitical, economic, and cultural
systems intertwine, forming a much more complex and nonlinear
map of society than in classical bourgeois models of the political nation. This, a kind of "civilizational turbulence," demands a nonlinear
approach and detailed description of each separate segment. In a civilization, the interdependence of social groups and strata forms a complex game of plural identities, superimposed on one another, coming
apart and together into new knots. A shared civilizational code (for
instance, religion) produces the frame conditions, but within these
borders there can be a significant degree of variation. Part of identity
can be based on tradition, but part is an innovative construction, since
civilization in the TMW is thought of as a living historical organism
in the process of constant transformations.

As in liberalism, the TMW recognizes behind the individuals of a
concrete civilization a non-zero degree of competence in international
questions, at least within the confines of the civilization. Individual
identity here is strictly marked by culture, and in this culture the
individual can always obtain the fundamental knowledge necessary
to form a point of view concerning concrete civilizational questions.
Thus, in the TMW on the individual level of an ordinary member of
society, we are most likely dealing with Rosenau's "skilled individual,"

rather than with the lambda-individual of realists: only the competence of this "skilled individual" is defined not by personal access to a
broad spectrum of non-codified information (as among transnationalists and globalists), but by belonging to a semantic field of tradition.

The Relevance of the English School to the TMW

The English School of IR is extremely productive for the construction
of a sociology of intercivilizational interaction. Representatives of this
school examined the sphere of international relations *as a society*, and,
accordingly, they gave priority to the study of the procedures and protocols of the socialization of countries in the sphere of international
relations, i.e. to international "socialization." They thereby supplied IR
theorists with an arsenal of methods, intended for the deep study of
the regularities of the interactions of actors in international relations.
In the TMW, the actors change: instead of states, they are civilizations.
At the same time, the structure of the sphere of international relations also changes. Accordingly, the methods of the English School
can be taken as a basis for studying the *intercivilizational socium*, the
ensemble of civilizations and the structures of dialogue occurring
among them.

The thesis of the "dialogue of civilizations" acquires in the English
School a concrete content: this dialogue can be thought of as a strategy
of socialization, a dynamic of gradient relations, rhythms of exclusion/
inclusion, attempts to hierarchize the system of relations, expansion
and retreat, protocols of war and peace, material and spiritual balance,
etc.

In a multipolar world, civilizations will be a planetary society,
required in one way or another to acknowledge *an other* alongside it.
But in this case the other will not be a state, but a civilization other
than the given one. How the figure of the other will be structured,
to what extent it will have negative and pejorative traits, and to what
extent it can be considered in the spirit of peaceful competition and

partnership, will depend on many factors, which it is not possible to foretell. But the conceptual instruments of the English School are theoretically wonderfully useful for further theory construction.

As an example we can take the model of the Islamic world in the contemporary West. A certain demonization of Islam as a civilization (especially after "9–11") became a characteristic civilizational cliché in the West (independent of what country is at issue and on what basis this negative model is formed, whether on the basis of Christian identity or pure secularism). Something analogous is characteristic also for Americaphobia and the general hostility toward the West in the Islamic world — and again, independently of what concrete state is at issue. We are dealing with a distribution of social statuses and roles on the level of international relations, and this to a significant extent is studied as a priority by the English School in IR, which puts at the center of attention the "society of states" and the social aspects of their interaction, inter-recognition, and inter-estimation.

The methods of the English School will be acceptable in the TMW. Instead of the "society of states" we will study "the society of civilizations" and the sociological processes occurring in this society.

The Relevance of Marxism and Neo-Marxism to the TMW

Marxism and neo-Marxism in IR are very useful for the TMW as a doctrinal arsenal for the critique of the universalism of Western civilization and its pretensions to moral superiority, based on the factor of material, technological, and financial superiority. Western civilization in modernity took the path of capitalism and reached the furthest horizons of this path. But the material embodiment of success on the highest level of economic development and effectiveness of market procedures, and in recent times in the high-priority development of the financial sector, can serve as a decisive argument only if we agree to accept capital as the standard not only of material, but also social, cultural, and spiritual values. Weber showed this wonderfully when he identified capitalism as the expression of the Protestant ethic, where man's reward during life by riches and success is regarded as a direct reflection of his moral worth. The sign of equality between prosperity and morality as a distinctive mark of the Western society of modernity thus has religious and cultural sources. Capital and capitalism prove to be not simply the standard of might, but the standard of right.

From the start, Marxism challenges this approach and, acknowledging the power of capital, denies it the right of moral superiority. Marxist ethics are arranged in a precisely opposite way. Good are labor and the laboring class (the proletariat), which under capitalism is fully enslaved by the parasite class of the bourgeoisie. "Rich" for Marxism means "bad." Consequently, material development or the concentration of capital in some countries or others does not simply prove nothing, but proves that at issue are the most unjust and hence wicked societies, which must be destroyed.

In IR analysis, this Marxist ethics leads to the moral evaluation of the "rich North" and the core of the capitalist world-system as the historic, geographic, social expression of global evil. The West becomes not a model for imitation and longing, a promised land, where all questions receive their answer, but as the citadel of exploitation, lies, violence, and injustice.

Without sharing dogmatically all the conclusions regarding world revolution and the messianic destiny of the proletariat, the TMW accepts the Marxist approach to the evaluation of the capitalist nature of the West and solidarizes with the denunciation of capitalism as an asymmetrical model of exploitation and the imposition of the West's civilizational criteria (capitalism, the free market, the pursuit of gain, materialism, consumerism, etc.) on all other peoples and societies. *Capitalism is the material, economic side of Western universalism and Western colonialism.* Accepting the logic of capital, we are automatically obligated sooner or later to recognize the West and its civilization as the reference point, the model for imitation, and the horizon of development. But this is directly opposed to the idea of a multipolar world order and to the value pluralism of civilizations. For some civilizations, material prosperity and capitalist forms of economy are acceptable and desirable, but for other civilizations it is possible that they are not at all so. Capitalism is not obligatory and is not the only form of organizing an economy. It can be accepted or refused. Identifying material prosperity with moral worth can be justified by some and rejected by others. Hence, for the TMW the anti-capitalist vector of Marxism and neo-Marxism in IR, and also the unmasking of exploitative procedures characteristic of dependent development, is an important element and can full well be accepted as a tool. The same thing is also suitable for the critique of the "rich North" and the call to oppose the core of the world system. Without this opposition, the emergence of a multipolar world is impossible.

The main difference between the TMW and neo-Marxism and world-systems theory (as well as the projects of Negri and Hardt and other alterglobalists) is that the TMW categorically rejects the historical fatalism of Marxist theories, which insist that capitalism is a universal and necessary phase of historical development, after which the proletarian revolution must follow, just as fatefully and necessarily. For the TMW, capitalism is an empirically fixed form of development of Western European civilization, which grew out of the roots of Western European culture and has acquired today an almost planetary scope. But a deep analysis of capitalism in non-Western societies shows that in them it has an entirely imitative and superficial character, possesses other semantic characteristics, and is always something special and distinct from the socio-economic formations that prevail in the contemporary West. Capitalism arose in the West, and there it can either develop further or die. But its expansion beyond the limits of the Western world, although conditional on capital's striving to grow, is completely unjustified from the perspective of the non-Western societies on which it is projected. Each civilization can have its own time, its own notion of history, its own vision of the economy and material development. Capitalism invades non-Western societies as a continuation of colonial practice, and, consequently, can and should be rejected, reversed, as the aggression of a foreign culture or foreign civilization. Hence, the TMW insists that the battle against the "rich North" should proceed today by all subjects of the political map of humanity, and especially the countries of the "Second World" (Wallerstein's semi-periphery). The multipolar world should come not *after liberalism* (as neo-Marxists think), but *instead of liberalism*. Thus, the battle against liberalism should be carried out not in the name of what comes after it once it has been consolidated on a global scale, but *already today*, so that it will never be consolidated on a global scale. It is not necessary for non-Western civilizations to pass through the capitalist phase of development. Just as it is not necessary to mobilize one's population for the proletariat revolution. The elites and masses of the countries of the "semi-periphery," contrary to neo-Marxists, are not at all required to separate and integrate into two international classes, the global proletariat and the global bourgeoisie, losing all their civilizational features. On the contrary, the elites and masses belonging to one or another civilization must recognize their shared civilizational identity, the significance of which should be weightier than the significance of class identity.

If, as regards the international solidarity of the bourgeoisie and (to a lesser extent) the proletariat, Marxists are sometimes right (since at issue are the capitalist societies and bourgeois states, where indeed the logic of capital prevails), appeal to some other, non-Western civilization qualitatively changes everything. The elites and masses of the Islamic world, for instance, are much more keenly aware of their shared belonging to Islamic culture than to their class proximity to the elites and masses of other civilizations, Western in particular. And this unity should not be washed out and shaken loose (by liberal cosmopolitanism and neo-Marxist or anarchist class internationalism), but consolidated, developed, and supported.

The multipolar world, especially in its first, anti-hegemonic phase, should be built on the solidarity of all civilizations in opposition to the colonial and globalist practices of the "rich North." And this struggle should rally elites and masses within the civilizations, the more so since applying purely class criteria to them (elites as bourgeoisie, masses as proletariat) is the projection of a Western hegemonic approach. In non-Western civilizations there are without doubt empirically higher and lower strata, but their sociological and cultural semantics differ significantly from the reductionist models, where the most important and sole criterion is relation to the ownership of the means of production. Hence, the TMW appeals to the civilizational solidarity of elites and masses in the shared construction of the pole of a multipolar world and the organization of a "large space" in accordance with the historical and cultural peculiarities of each separate society.

The Relevance of Critical Theory to the TMW

Postpositivist IR theories are very productive for the TMW.

IR critical theory can be put to work practically in its entirety for the denunciation of Western hegemony. The critique of West-centric pretensions, global capitalism, liberal globalization, and the unipolar world in this theory correspond to the main attitudes of the TMW and are a necessary part of it. Without clear recognition of the hegemonic nature of the present system of international relations and its essential unipolarity (however it might be expressed — directly, indirectly, or tacitly), the need for an alternative cannot be justified. The TMW represents from the start a radical alternative to precisely the existing hegemony. Thus, the detailed and thorough description of its structures, its methods of consolidation, and its concealment of its essence, as well as its unmasking, are very important elements of the TMW. Critical theory in IR (Cox, in the first place) is a model of such a frontal attack, the main points of which can be fully integrated into the TMW. This concerns both the structuralist and the linguistic analysis of hegemony.

The conception, stemming from the critique of hegemony, of a contra-hegemonic bloc can be taken into the ammunition of the TMW. At the same time, the concept of a contra-hegemonic bloc acquires in the TMW more concrete and systemized features than in the inertially Marxist critical theory. *The contra-hegemonic bloc in the TMW is the totality of those powers in all presently existing civilizations which recognize the current state of hegemony as unacceptable and failing to meet the interests of peoples and societies.* The core of the contra-hegemonic bloc should be avant-garde intellectuals, who represent the main civilizations that claim to be an independent pole, which under the present hegemonic conditions is harshly denied them *a priori*: Orthodox (Eurasian), Islamic, Chinese, Hindu, Latin American (and also Buddhist, Japanese, and African). Within Western civilization it is also entirely possible for intellectual circles to unite in that regard Western civilization (American and European) as *local and regional* and prefer to limit the zone of their expansion by their historical limits (supporters of American isolation or the project "Fortress Europe"). On the second level, the core of the contra-hegemonic bloc can be all the forces that oppose globalization and the unipolar world on some other basis, for instance, class, ethnic, cultural, religious, or ideological. But if we take into account that in the construction of a contra-hegemonic bloc the supporters of a multipolar world, the whole family of intellectuals and theoreticians, will rely on the gigantic potential of their civilizations and not only on the moral rejection of hegemony, this bloc will instantly transform into something much more serious than we can imagine if we take into account only our impressions from the texts and suggestions of Western theorists, who as a rule represent non-conformist and marginal groups. Dialogue with contra-hegemonists of all types, belonging to all groups and cultural zones, is, undoubtedly, extremely important, but the priority is consolidation of precisely the members of the strong and regionally sound civilizational powers.

Only in combination with the TMW does critical theory transform from a noble intellectual game and morally heroic position into an imposing political force.

The Relevance of Postmodern Theory to the TMW

No less important is postmodernism in IR, first of all for the systematic deconstruction of the power discourse with the help of which Western hegemony presents itself as something natural, without alternatives, and alone possible. The entire structure of the theorization of the field of international relations in Western political science, to say nothing of the political discourses concerning international questions among Western politicians, is a well-organized field of "self-fulfilling prophecies," "problem-solving theories," and "wishful thinking." IR theories and the global discourse of Western leaders is a kind of "neuro-linguistic programming," called on to impose on humanity through text the model of reality that is always organized to satisfy the interests of the Western elite. Knowledge, postmodernists in IR emphasize, cannot be objective and neutral. And the exposure of whom and what one or another theory serves is the unique and extremely useful instrument of deconstruction in IR. Sometimes this act is called "subversive," since it helps to highlight the strained arguments, figures of omission, and double standards, with which are replete theoretical texts and all the more so political declarations describing the logic of processes in international relations and thereby predetermining them. On the whole, postmodernists follow the same line as critical theorists, unmasking and exhibiting the hegemonic nature of the West and its "totalitarian" discourse, used to impose Western interests and values on all other societies, despite the fact that the population of the West represents a minority of humanity and its culture is neither the most ancient nor the most perfect (if we can apply a value-scale to civilizations at all).

Postmodernism in IR is extremely useful also in getting out from under the prejudices of "empiricism," "verification," "statistical significance," etc., characteristic residues of the overcome belief of the modern epoch in the independent ontological object. On the level of the philosophy of science and sociology, the idea that the criterion of scienticity is the verifiability of the fact in practice has long since been refuted and replaced by other, more precise criteria, falsification in particular (Popper, Lakatos), i.e. the recognition as scientific of a hypothesis that can be disposed of by a rational system of proofs. Other epistemologists spoke of "paradigm shifts" (Kuhn) or the "proliferation of hypotheses" (Feyerband) as the main signs of scienticity. These philosophical elaborations were introduced into IR later, but postmodernists remedy this shortcoming, bringing the self-reflection of IR specialists to the required level. In postmodern epistemology, there are no facts, objects, or subjects. There are only processes, aleatory codes, structures, networks, hybrids (Latour) or rhizomes (Deleuze). And they can all either organize around the axis of the will to power or weaken and be left to themselves.

Here we can mark one important difference between IR postmodernism and the TMW. So long as at issue is the critique of Western hegemony and the West's will to power through unmasking structures of domination and establishing inequalities on the level of discourse and theory, both theories go hand in hand. The TMW fully acknowledges the arsenal of postmodern criticism and borrows its basic methods of deconstruction. The deconstruction of hegemony is accepted fully. The difference begins where postmodernists advance their alternative project. It amounts most often to the demand for complete repudiation of the "will to power" altogether, from any hierarchy, and appeal to a general, relaxed chaos, in which any hierarchical geometry of being, knowledge, society, politics, materiality, gender, production practices, etc., dies out and is erased. Deconstructing the power of the West, postmodernists strive thereby to overthrow the principle of hierarchy altogether. The TMW does not share this pathos. It thinks that the deconstruction of the "will to power" of the West is very useful for clearing the field for the creation of a TMW, and, accordingly, for the construction of a multipolar world as such. It does not get rid of the "will to power" as a phenomenon, and with it any hierarchical geometry of the world, but relativizes this will, demonopolizes the West in its pretensions to being the sole bearer of the "will to power" and imposing its Western (today, liberal-capitalist) version of this will on everyone else.

The Western "will to power" exists, and it really predetermines the structure of the entire Western discourse. The sphere of IR and its theoretical comprehension is organized in accordance with this (more precisely, comprehension organizes this sphere *through* its theoretical comprehension [*osmyslenie organizuet etu sredu cherez yeye teoreticheskoe osmyslenie*]). But after revealing and acknowledging this, we can draw conclusions different from those that postmodernists draw. Without denying this will altogether, we should limit it by the natural historical and geographic limits of Western civilization and allow it within these limits to either assert itself, transform itself, or slide into the networks and tubers of turbulent society. This is a choice for the West. But the choice for other civilizations — Eurasian, Islamic, Chinese, Hindu, etc. — can well consist in *defending the right to cultivate their own version of the "will to power," built on the basis of historical traditions, cultures, religions, social particularities, etc.* The Orthodox, Chinese, Islamic, or Hindu versions of the "will to power" might differ from each other and from the European one, and each of them has every reason to secure, change, mutate, or scatter. *In each civilization, the "will to power" can have its own fate.* After freeing themselves from the global influence of the hegemonic discourse of the West and compulsion to its full imitation (to the point of a caricature), civilizations will receive a tremendous degree of freedom to act with the autochthonous structures of the "will to power" according to their own discretion. But here, too, there should be no universal pretensions (including postmodern ones). The "will to power" can be accepted or rejected; this is up to each concrete society. But it is necessary to become free from the sole hegemonic "will to power" of the modern capitalist West.

The Relevance of Feminist Theory to the TMW

Feminism in IR has great methodological value for the TMW inasmuch as it demonstrates how sociological position (in this case, gender position) affects theoretical constructs. Especially valuable is standpoint feminism, which clearly proves the possibility of a radical reconsideration of sociopolitical theories if they are built in a different sociological starting point; in this case, not from the male, but from the female "standpoint." As a result, we get an entirely distinct theory, having little in common with what is generally accepted. Thus, pretensions to universality of one-sided (here: masculine) discourses are undermined. The TMW suggests repeating this approach, placing at the basis of theory not another gender, but another civilizational identity. This gives us a "standpoint civilizational approach." If for Western civilization Hobbes's anthropological principle "man is a wolf to man" can work and become the foundation for further political science constructions, right up to the concept of the Leviathan, sovereignty, the nation-state, and the anarchy of international relations, or can be contested by the more humane and pacifistic positions of Locke and Kant, then in the context of any other civilization we are dealing with an entirely different anthropology, connected with essentially different basic notions of the human and human nature.

For instance, in Hinduism the principle operates that "man is God to man"; in Orthodox ethics, that "you are greater than I"; and in the Islamic religion, "there are no differences between one and another before Allah." Everywhere, different realities serve as the measure of things; somewhere everything is measured by man; *somewhere else, not*, and man is thought of as derived from a different substance (for instance, in Buddhism the individual is an accidental stream of intertwining *dharmas* and does not have his own nature or "I," hence the Buddhist principle of *anātman*.)

We should take some concrete anthropological *point of view*, but not that of Western civilization, and we will get an entirely new conception of the state, power, society, history, and international and interstate relations and ties, differing much more from the Western one than the male perspective does from the female one within the framework of Western civilization. So feminism in IR can serve as an illustration of the sociological pluralism of starting positions, which can be applied in an entirely new context.

As for the demand of feminists to broaden the presence of the female principle in IR theorizing, precisely this is not necessarily reproduced in the TMW.

Besides the fact that male and female perspectives on the world vary significantly in the context of one or another civilization (which feminists rightly indicate, suggesting that we study and take these variations into account), *different civilizations construct the gender pair in different ways*, also on the basis of a unique anthropology peculiar to them. For instance, depriving the Hindu woman of the right to enter a sacrificial fire voluntarily after the death of her husband (the *sati* rite), fixed in the legislation of contemporary India, which copied the legal codes of Western countries, can full well be considered an "infringement of the rights of the Hindu woman," while among Europeans of both sexes this rite will likely only inspire horror and aversion. In different civilizations, the semantic content of gender differs fundamentally, and the question of the place of women in society should be resolved on the basis of local social traditions and foundations.

If feminists fight against men's efforts to pass off their gender archetypes and attitudes as something universal, they should judge in the same way the attempt to pass off as universal any values with a historical and local origin, including the idea of the equality of sexes, which in its contemporary form is an undoubtedly purely Western, modern, and partially postmodern concept.

The Relevance of Historical Sociology to the TMW

Also highly relevant for the TMW is the method of historical sociology in IR, since it allows us to examine the contemporary evolution of the entire system of international relations in a historical perspective and thus to broaden the horizons of the future and make possible a new, deeper comprehension of history. The members of this school in IR criticize classical theories for their lack of a historical dimension. This means that these theories do not pay enough attention to the *evolution* of actors, acting units, and leading principles that predetermine the interactions of states and societies in various historical stages. Thinking that today's state of affairs in one way or another repeats what has always been, and projecting the present status quo onto the past (the tempocentrism and chronocentrism of the majority of IR theories), classical IR paradigms close the possibility of understanding the past and condemn the future to repeat the same mechanical regularities. The loss of the historical sense leads the majority of IR theorists to inadequate prognoses and analyses, a clear case of which is the total inability of neorealists and neoliberals to predict the collapse of the bipolar world and the fall of the USSR literally right before these fundamental events became realized facts.

The structure of international relations was once qualitatively different from what it is now, and it is entirely likely that in the near future it will become qualitatively different from what exists today. To predict and project the future and to understand the past, specific theoretical tools are necessary in the sphere of IR, which historical sociology develops. One version of a historico-sociological approach is offered by the famous theoreticians of this approach, Buzan and Little. They introduce the concept of an "international system" and trace the fundamental changes of this system in various historical stages. The essence of their theory amounts to the following. There are four kinds of "international system":

- *the pre-national system* (characteristic of those societies where there are still no traces of political statehood: tribes of hunters and gatherers, the earliest phases of agricultural production, etc);

- *the classical or ancient system* (corresponds to city-states, empires, and the first political formations; this system is characteristic of traditional societies and continued to exist for centuries, right up to the start of modernity in Europe);

- *the global international system* (replaces the classical; is based on the interactions of sovereign nation-states and is characterized by the fact that it casts the net of national territories over the entire inhabited space of the planet, hence its global character);

- *the postmodern international system* (which forms as a result of globalization and is a result of the mutations of the previous system and the diffusion of the structures of the nation-state).

In the transition from one international system to another, practically everything changes: the main actors, the structure of interactions among them, the intensity of contacts and exchanges, the economic order, the political form of power, ideology, etc. At the same time, all historical transitions occur not simultaneously and not instantly, but sometimes over millennia, and at different speeds in various parts of the world. In order to understand the present moment in international relations, it is necessary to situate it in a concrete, fundamental historico-sociological context.

The theory of international systems is important for the TMW for two reasons. First, this theory allows us to understand better how the emergence of civilization as candidate for the main actor of international relations becomes possible. Second, in its context it is possible to focus on the historical and sociological meaning of what will become of the postmodern system; after all, today it is entirely unclear in what direction it will evolve; moreover, the most serious disagreements over this direction can and should arise. The future is not predetermined. It is open and is made by those who make a decision today. Let us look at this aspect more closely.

If we follow universalist and West-centric views of history, the transition to a global international system is something "irreversible" and "just" for all societies of the world. Even where countries were originally included in this system as European *colonies*, they gradually receive independence and acquire national sovereignty. But that is only how things stand superficially. Under the thin film of the modernization of the political systems in the majority of non-Western countries, an entirely different sociocultural model is preserved, corresponding as a rule to precisely the classical or ancient international system. Modernization is spread over the top layers of society, but the majority remain in a condition of traditional society. Thus, the former colonial societies that received independence are only formally "sovereign," and, accordingly, only formally full-fledged actors of the Westphalian system. Essentially, they remain traditional societies, as before.

Precisely this factor becomes apparent when a bipolar world collapses. From under the thin veneer of modernization, the contours of the *real content* of many sociocultural regions appear. Here one detects the increasing significance and role of all the indicators that comprise the distinct features of traditional society: religion, ethics, the family, the ethnos, eschatology, etc. This is the phenomenon of the "emergence of civilizations," when after the collapse of the structure of modernity (bipolarity), the content of premodernity arises (the clash or dialogue of civilizations).

In the terms of the historical sociology approach in IR, this is described as the disclosure of the signs of a *classical* international system in the transition from a *global* international system to a *postmodern* one. The globalizing world, intending to take a decisive step forward beyond the bounds of modernity, suddenly discovers that in many regions of the world modernity has, it seems, plainly not yet even been approved and the modern era has not begun. And here the suspicion arises that maybe in these non-Western societies modernity in its customary European understanding is altogether impossible, and the modern era will never begin. This is the actor civilization, with all its premodern attributes. And if this actor is sufficiently strong and stable, the universalist and progressivist logic of the linear understanding of history, characteristic of the West, will be overthrown. The TMW in a certain sense proposes to carry this out, moving from the linear understanding of history to a cyclical one, from the common and single time of humanity to the special trajectories and paths of separate civilizational times, criss-crossing with one another in a complex and constantly changing pattern, demanding fixed attention.

From here, we can take a further step and consider the postmodern international system, about which Buzan and Little speak, as an open *choice* between continuing West-centric globalization, but only with the constant blurring of the vertical orientation of the hegemonic discourse of the West, and the multipolar project, in which there come into play forgotten, but newly awakening from anabiosis, *structures of traditional society*, i.e. civilizations, cultures, religions. If in the context of each international system meanings, actors, ties, and structures change, then the transition from the global system to the new system also implies shifts, demolitions, and replacements of identities and paradigms. It is not correct to apply modern criteria that have clearly lost their relevance to the postmodern system. But this means that the semantic horizons of the international system that is coming to replace the global system and is for now conditionally defined as "postmodern" remain open and problematic, and various segments of humanity can put up a tense and passionate fight for their formulation.

This is an important point of the TMW: postmodernism in IR is not predetermined and does not signify the transition from one approximately understood structure of international relations to another, also apprehended on the whole. It is rather an open process with uncertain outcomes, which can lead to one model of a world order, or to a completely different one with its own parameters. The postmodern can be the continuation of the modern, or it can represent an exit beyond the limits of the main logic of its development. This second variant of postmodernity provides a chance to built a multipolar world on the basis of civilizational pluralism.

Another highly important theoretical point for the development of the TMW is the critique by members of the school of historical sociology (Hobson in particular) of the eurocentrism and racism of all existing theories of IR. His book *The Eurocentric Conception of World Politics* is a fundamental theoretical contribution to the emergence of the TMW and can be wholly included in the context of this theory. On one hand, Hobson demonstrates the groundlessness of the identification of the Western system of values as universal, so that the Western system is announced as the highest and all other civilizational types and their value systems as lower (direct or subliminal racism), and, on the other hand, he proposes to construct a balanced and polycentric theory of IR, where Western civilization would be returned to its historical and "provincial" (from the perspective of the entire planet and all humanity) context. Hobson's ideas can be fully integrated into the TMW and can become its most important conceptual element.

The Relevance of Normativism to the TMW

Normativism in IR is very convenient for the "thick" analysis of civilizations and the structure of relations and ties among them. This approach puts at the center of attention the study of the norms, values, ideas, and ideals of concrete societies, with the help of which one attains a deep understanding of how the main themes of international relations are conceived of in various countries and social contexts. The normativistic approach suggests that each society conceives of and interprets models of world politics in accordance with cultural attitudes (norms). And these norms influence the political leadership and other centers of decision-making in foreign policy, since they are never torn out of the rest of the social milieu, but are connected with it and depend on it because of domestic considerations (the question of legitimacy). If separate lambda-individuals, and even a plurality of them, lack competence in the sphere of international relations and in questions of foreign policy, their joint ideas can full well influence the legitimacy of the rules. Foreign policy is thus placed in a concrete sociocultural context, and in this context symbols, preferences, attitudes, and ethnic complexes play an important role.

In giving priority attention to models in the sphere of international relations (for instance, the figure of the "other") and their resonance in a concrete society, normativists bring us right up to the composition of the civilizational map, where different societies project onto the international domain different complexes of moral criteria, ethnic assessments, imperatives, and rules. How this combines with concrete actual policies in each concrete case should be examined separately, but with this approach the entire sphere of zones of international relations becomes not a space for the application of power and economic technologies or institutional globalistic initiatives, but a field of symbols and signs, which different cultures and societies interpret differently, in accordance with their value-complexes.

Thus, opened up for the TMW is the broad expanse of *the symbolic analysis of international relations* on the basis of concrete civilizational ensembles, each of which is described though an original picture of norms and ideals.

Another valuable aspect of normativism is the distinction between two ethical systems in IR, drawn in the works of the normativist Brown. The TMW starts from the fact that under multipolarity only a communitarian ethic should be regarded as normative, since each civilization bases its value system on its own criteria and principles, and even "universality" is understood differently each time, i.e. locally. The absence of a measure common to all civilizations, following from the civilizational relativism of the TMW, precludes the possibility of a grounded cosmopolitan ethic. And that which is advanced as such an ethic is upon closer examination found to be the *universalization of the Western civilizational model*. Thus, universalism and the globalism based on it prove to be only forms of colonialism, imperialism, and racism, i.e. the projection by one communitarian (historically and geographically predetermined) ethical system on all humanity.

The Relevance of Constructivism to the TMW

We have already spoken of the significance of constructivism for the TMW earlier. Most important in this approach is the attention given to *theoretical constructions*, which often have a special significance in the accomplishment of some or another project. Ideas about the world affect the world, and if they do not make it into the way it is thought about, they at least impart to it certain qualitative features. Consequently, the system of international relations is to a large extent a *result of construction* in the process of unfolding the theoretical field of IR as a discipline.

Constructivists themselves, Wendt in the first place, prefer to use this method in a humanistic, neoliberal spirit, pointing to the fact that much in IR depends on self-limiting formulations or conflicts pre-programmed by initial attitudes. Wendt thinks that the anarchy of international relations can be interpreted variously — in the spirit of Hobbes (competition, preparedness for war), in the spirit of Locke (competition, peaceful contest), and in the spirit of Kant (solidarity, partnership, uniting into a single civil society). According to Wendt, this is ontologically one and the same anarchy, but its gnoseological evaluation allows it to be constructed on the basis of a field of enmity, a zone of competition, or a space of close cooperation in solidarity.

How we configure our understanding of reality in international relations is how it will finally turn out. According to constructivists, we live in the world we ourselves create. Nicholas Onuf formulates this idea in the title of his book, *World of Our Making*.

But in the context of the TMW, we can draw on the basis of the constructive notion of the nature of international relations a conclusion that differs from the (on the whole) liberal orientation of constructivists themselves. They want to make the world "more humane" in the sense of a greater correspondence with the values they take as basic and self-evident in the context of Western modern and in part postmodern culture. But this is a "world of their making." Non-Western civilizations fully logically prefer to "*make the world*" in accordance with their own attitudes and ideas, traditions and cultural patters. The Western world, claiming today to be the sole and universal model of the world, is *made by the people of the West.* They learned to deconstruct it and constitute it anew. This practice is critically important for the TMW. But it should be applied a new context and to resolve different problems. Having recognized that in the norms claiming self-evidence and universalism (technological progress, democracy, human rights, tolerance, humanism, the market economy, the free press, etc.) we are *dealing with the projections of only one civilization*, what's more, with features inherent to only one historical phase of this civilization, we will be able to easily localize Western discourse, deconstruct it and *free thereby a semantic field for the construction of another reality.* The world made by us, not them, can and should be multipolar. And to become so, it remains only to be constructed.

We should begin with theory, since the sources of what we start to apprehend and experience as a reality, a fact, and the status quo, begin precisely in the space of representations and concepts.

An Example of the Analysis of a Multipolar World in Comparison with the Postmodern International System

The proposed analysis of the international system leads to the distinction of the following levels:

- system
- subsystem
- unit
- subunit
- individual

And to the examination of their relations:

- military
- political
- economic
- social
- ambient.

Also distinguished in an international system are

- *interaction* (it can be linear or multiordinate, which determines the intensity of the interactions, which most often reduce to five types: war, union, trade, borrowing, and domination);
- *structure* (the static model of organizing the unit in the system);
- *process* (the qualitative transformation of all relations).

According to Buzan and Little, the postmodern international system is characterized by the following features:

- expanding the list of basic units (compared to the global system, where the predominant actors were states);

- the emergence of non-state actors, right up to new units, asphalt nomads (Jünger, Attali), the cosmopolitan entirely indifferent to the system of territorialized hierarchies;

- an even greater intensity of interrelations;

- the rise of new supranational spaces — information spaces, trade spaces, cultural spaces, network spaces, spaces of distribution, style spaces;

- global interaction as dispersion (the dispersion of basic military-political units into trade-economic units);

- the emergence of new localities (regionalism).

This picture of the postmodern international system, described by Buzan and Little, corresponds on the whole to the globalist vision and to the concepts of transnationalism and neoliberalism.

Now let us describe by the same method the multipolar world. The global *basic unit* is the civilization (the poles of a multipolar world). This unit enters into a global system, based on *intercivilizational interaction*. A subsystem forms with the neighbouring civilization, different each time depending on the civilization. There can be asymmetrical situations here. On the level of *sub-units*, we encounter a spectrum of concepts, and the list of them can vary and be asymmetrical — partially hierarchical, partially juxtaposed.

In the postmodern system, there is a coincidence here with multipolarity: in both there is a growth in the significance of local factors and a new regionalism. Thus, among *subunits*, we can distinguish the *dominant* sociocultural community and *minority* communities. These minority communities can correspond to the dominant communities of other civilizations, or they can be unique. These communities can be structured by cultural, religious, ethnic, territorial, or other indicators, forming a *superimposition* of identities. Each of these identities can be identical to or differ from the dominant community and can have or lack a counterpart in other civilizations. Intercivilizational relations will take shape accordingly.

The emergence of new or reemergence of old communities (religious, ethnic, sociocultural, and others) is a feature of the multipolar world.

Relations among civilizations will form irregularly depending on what subunit we consider. Ties with separate religious or sociocultural groups can develop very intensively. Among the dominant groups of civilizations, by contrast, ties and exchanges will likely be carried out in a rather limited sphere and through the mediation of specially appointed intermediaries.

Instead of increasing the role of the individual actor, the asphalt nomad, multipolarity proposes to reduce individual identity to a minimum in favor of a diverse choice of asymmetric collective identities and sets of social statuses.

The phenomenon of technology, claiming to be universal and culturally neutral, will be returned to its original historico-cultural context and recognized as a specific gadget of only one civilization, as an expression of its hegemonic pretensions and ethnocentric impulse.

Comparing the models of the postmodern system, put forward by historical sociologists in IR (and shared on the whole by transnationalists, globalists, and neoliberals), with the model of a multipolar world, we see fundamental differences in the picture of the future. In one case (among typical postmodernists), we are dealing with the transpositions of the contemporary Western code onto a more and more atomized *individual* level. In the second case, humanity recombines and reorganizes on the basis of *holism* — collective identity, although the structure of this identity, the interactions among various groups and processes, reflecting the constant change of these interactions, will be dynamic, not reducible to the classical international system, the global one, or the one that historical sociologists in IR call "postmodern," in their neoliberal and transnational versions.

At the same time, the significant semantic dimension of the nature of the unit in comparison with the global system, where the basic unit was the nation-state, can in the TMW be likened to the difference between the elementary particles of classical physics and fractals (Mandelbrot) or loops (in Witten's superstring theory). *Civilization is a complex reality with a very complicated and always unique geometry* and a system of strange attractors. Hence, the system of international relations—such as war, union, exchange, borrowing, and domination—also acquires a *complex* character. Intercivilizational war will be something fundamentally different from wars between states, in essence and in form. Also different will be the union of civilizations or the nature of peace agreements. The character of exchange, including economic exchange, will be defined by the level on which these operations occur: in a civilization, these can be rather diverse authorities and groups (in contrast to the state-centric conception in the classical paradigms of IR or atomic individuals and groups in neoliberalism and neo-Marxism).

Finally, the dominance of one civilization over another can also have an ambivalent character: material superiority will not always imply cognitive superiority and gnoseological hegemony. And, by contrast, spiritual dominance can in separate cases be accompanied by a lag in material development. The multipolar world leaves all possibilities maximally open. We can draw an important conclusion from this: the multipolar world is the space of maximally open history, where the animated participation of societies in the creation of a new world, a new map of reality, will not be limited by any external bounds, any hegemony, any reductionism or universalism, any rules pre-established or imposed by some side. This multipolar reality will be much more complex, complicated, and multidimensional than any postmodern intuitions.

The multipolar world is a manufactured space of practically un-
limited historical freedom, the freedom of peoples and communities
themselves to make their own history.

Summary

The following table summarizes the main similarities and differences
between the TMW and other paradigms of IR:

Paradigm	Similarities	Differences
Realism	Sovereignty of actors; anarchy of international relations	Actor is not the nation-state but civilization / *politeia*
Neorealism	Balance of powers; hegemony	Rejects the global hegemony of the West; rejects bipolarity
Liberalism	Integration and supranational institutionalization on the basis of shared values	Rejects the priority of liberal democracy; denies the universality of Western values
Neoliberalism	-	Rejects globalization and transnationalism
Marxism / Neo-Marxism	The critique of global capitalism	Denies the universality of phases of development; rejects the necessity of a global world-system
Critical Theory	The critique of Western and capitalist hegemony; contra-hegemony	Rejects individualism, marginalism, anarchism as values (contra-social)
Postmodernism	Deconstructing the global will to power	Rejects the devaluation of the will to power as such

Feminism	Deconstructing gender masculinism and exclusivism in IR; taking female gender into account in culture and civilization; standpoint feminism	Rejects liberal feminism, straightforward egalitarianism, the legalization of same-sex marriage, the relativization and deontologization of sex
Historical Sociology	Anti-racism; anti-Eurocentrism; the historicity of societies and international systems; the critique of tempocentrism and chronocentrism; building non-Western IR theory	-
Normativism	The priority of norms and values in defining civilizations; communitarian ethic	Rejects cosmopolitan ethic
Constructivism	The constructed character of the object of IR; deconstruction / reconstruction	Rejects subliminal Eurocentrism

5

The Main Themes and Topics of IR in the Context of the TMW

Authority (the Prince) in the TMW

LET US LOOK at a few concrete aspects of the TMW as applied to classical topics studied by IR.

A very important question in IR is the identification of the instance that will be the bearer of the supreme authority, determining the structure of the actor's behaviour in the sphere of international relations. This instance is functionally called "the bearer of sovereignty," or "the Prince" (in the terminology of Machiavelli).

The *basic unit* in the TMW is, as we saw, the *civilization*. Accordingly, it is necessary to identify how the problem of authority and its bearer, and hence the problem of sovereignty, is solved in this case.

This question is not as simple as it might first appear. A civilization, as we saw, is a *complex* phenomenon, the mathematical and geometrical description of which demands the introduction of non-linearity. This is a fundamental difference between the civilization and the nation-state, which was introduced in modernity as a rationalized, schematized reduction of reality, such as it is regarded in the majority of IR theories. Only postpositivist IR theories started to gradually relativize this linear picture, which dominates in realism and liberalism, and also with some significant modifications, in Marxism. The non-linearity of processes and complexity of actors in turbulent models of postmodern international relations looks primitive, simple, and predictable in comparison to civilizations. Postpostivitist theories have in any case as their conceptual limit the individual (hence the ideology of human rights), toward whose mathematical summation under all conditions the entire system of IR leads, even in the boldest postmodern models. The atomic individual is the conceptual basis of both nation-states and the postmodern alterglobalist multitudes. But in all cases this atomic individual is represented on the basis of Western anthropology and conceptualized in light of classic modern and postmodern ideas.

In other words, the limit of the complexity of turbulent systems is the individual as a concept, constructed in accordance with the patterns of Western European sociology. Correspondingly, all calculations around the problems of the bearer of sovereignty are in one way or another built on the basis of this concept. Atoms can be combined in the most fantastical and ingenious manner, but any composition will always amount to a digital code, subject to statistical calculation.

Thus, the question of authority and government in classical and even postpositivist IR theories can be reduced in principle to a calculational scheme: individuals and groups of individuals can delegate authority to their representatives right up to a sovereign ruler (individual or collective, a president, prime minister, government, parliament, etc.) or, by contrast, can move this authority lower and lower: to the middle (the subsidiarity of federal models, local self-government) or even lower, to the individual level (the project of the electronic referendum of all citizens through direct online participation in ultra-democratic utopias of planetary civil society). Whatever the instance of sovereignty, it is calculated and determined on the basis of the individual as a specifically Western basic sociological and anthropological concept. Authority is a human and individual phenomenon. But the pluralism of civilizations knocks the ground out from under such a conceptualization. The issue is that different civilizations operate with different anthropological constructs, the majority of which are not resolved into atomic individuals. In other words, atomic individuals are not irresolvable (atomic) or autonomously substantial elements. In different civilizations, man can be as you please, only not a self-dependent, self-identical unit. He is most often a conscious and explicit *function of the social whole* (this idea is the basis of the sociology of Durkheim and his followers, the cultural anthropology of Boas and his students, and also the structuralism of Levi-Strauss). Accordingly, the structure of authority and its formalization in each distinct civilization reflects the specific organization of a *holistic ensemble*, which can differ significantly in each concrete case.

The Hindu caste principle has little in common with Islamic religious democracy or Chinese ritualism. Moreover, the same civilizational bases can produce diverse conceptualizations of power in their relations to other societies and separate people. In Christian civilization we see at least two polar medieval models of the normative state: 1) the symphony of authorities and Caesaropapism of Byzantium (of which there are still echoes in Orthodox countries, especially in Russia) and 2) Augustinian, in the sense of the teaching of "two cities," the principle of the primacy of the Bishop of Rome, characteristic of the Catholic West. After the Reformation, a broad spectrum of Protestant conceptions of the nature of authority were added to this, from Lutheran monarchy to prophetic-liberal Calvinism and eschatological Anabaptism.

Hence, we should examine authority in the context of a civilization as a fractal, non-linear phenomenon, reflecting the distinctive geometry of each concrete social *holos*.

Of course, someone in a civilization must decide questions concerning intercivilizational relations, concerning, in particular, war and peace, union and its dissolution, cooperation and exchange, prohibitions, quotas, tariffs, etc. We can call this the *strategic pole* of civilization. This instance is conditional and advanced purely theoretically as a conceptual space where the decisions are concentrated that touch to some extent the sphere of international relations. This strategic pole is the pole of the multipolar world, inasmuch as the world of civilizations is opened as multipolar precisely because of the intersection of interests or formulation of interests occurring through *the instance of the pole.*

The strategic pole *must* be present in any civilization. Its presence makes the world multipolar, but its place and its content, and also its structure and ties with other levels of authority in each civilization can be unique and not resemble anything.

An example of one such complex system is the model of decision-making in contemporary Iran, where the extent of sovereignty is shared proportionally between the secular authority of the President and the spiritual structures of the Ayatollahs. In Saudi Arabia, the Majlis, an analogue of Parliament, is a field for consensual decisions by the three powers dominating in that society: the large royal family, the spiritual authorities of Salafi Islam, and the members of the more significant Bedouin tribes. In contemporary China, the collection of political and economic interests of this singular country in its movement into the sphere of international relations is strictly controlled and regulated by the Communist Party. In India, the balance of front-end secular parliamentarism and an implicit caste system produces a multilevel model for important decision-making. In Russia, paternal authoritarianism, barely concealed by Western-style democratic procedures, is fully stable.

All these real forms of the organization of the strategic pole are considered by Western measures "anomalous," liable to "Europeanization," "Westernization," "modernization," and "democratization," and then abolition in a general system of global civil society. But today this project seems increasingly utopian, even to the most

consistent apologists of planetary democracy. Significant in this regard is Fukuyama's change of opinion in recent years, as he recognized
that his expectations for a quick "end of history" were clearly too
hasty, since on the path to globalization and the creation of a planetary liberal-democratic system there are too many difficult obstacles
standing in the way of "placing the end of history" in the near future.

In taking up the model of the multipolar world, systems of authority rooted in the civilizational peculiarities of traditional societies *will
lose the necessity of concealing themselves* under superficially adopted
and equivocal Western democratic standards. Thus, the strategic pole
of civilization can announce itself fully openly, explicitly acknowledging itself as what it is implicitly in the majority of non-Western societies. But instead of feeling "remorse" for this before the unattainable
model of the West (advanced as a universal norm), civilizations get
the possibility of institutionalizing their own models of authority in
accordance with their own traditions, the historical condition of their
societies, and the will of the social figures, those exponents of the cultural *holos*, who are considered the most authoritative and competent
for such acts. This gives rise to the concept of "our Prince," *princeps
nostrum*, i.e. not simply a distinctive form of arranging the highest
authority (autocracy, democracy, government, dynasty, meritocracy,
etc.), but also freedom to saturate it with diverse civilizational content:
secular, sacred, functional, rational, or religious.

The civilizational pluralism of the TMW does not at all insist on
the abolition of democracy where it exists or on hindering its emergence and growth where it does not exist or is weak and nominal.
Nothing of the sort. The TMW is not anti-democratic. But it is also
not normatively democratic, since many civilizations and societies do
not at all consider democracy in its Western version a value or the
optimal form of sociopolitical organization. If this is what a society
thinks and if this has a foundation in the civilizational mode of life,
it should be adopted as a fact. Supporters of democracy can fight for

their ideals and opinions as much as they would like to. They can win, but they can also lose.

These are all questions that should be decided within a civilization, without taking account of reproachful, encouraging, or dissatisfied external reactions.

Thus, the strategic pole, which must exist because of the polycentric character of the multipolar world, cannot have a homogeneous political content, analogous to the concept of a nation-state in the Westphalian system. That system was based on optimistic confidence in the universality of human reason, by which was understood, as later became clear, the entirely *specific rationality* of the European human of the modern era, arrogantly and presumptuously taken as "transcendental reason" as such. The European rationality of the modern era, speedily eliminating itself today, proved to be a spatially *local historical moment*, nothing more. Postmodernism in general and the erosion of the Westphalian system in particular are connected with the gradual realization of this fact.

The TMW does not propose a new universalism in the domain of determining who should be the normative bearer of authority in the new basic units of a multipolar world. But it also does not fall into the chaotic ecstasy of the semi-animal rhizomatic irrationalism of post-structuralists. Civilizations as structures, as languages, have every ground to develop their own original models of rationality, the hierarchical symmetry of which, predetermining the structure of relations among authorities, and consequently the political arrangement of society (which is nothing but the trace of a philosophical paradigm, as Plato and Aristotle clearly show) can be of any kind.

So the question of authority in a multipolar world is answered as follows. From the outside, we mark in each civilization a strategic center, which acts as the subject of dialogue in international relations. This strategic center is the formalization of the civilization in its *metonymic abbreviation* in the system of multipolarity. But its structure and its content, its correlation with the internal layers and levels of society, the dimensions of its competence and the character of its legitimacy — all this can vary qualitatively and fundamentally. Multipolarity forbids evaluating this legitimacy from without, i.e. making a judgment about the content of authority in a civilization other than the one to which the observer belongs. Thus, the concept of a strategic center remains *fully concrete externally*, in the sphere of international relations, but *entirely arbitrary internally*, and it can be configured in accordance with the cultural codes of each separate society on the basis of the social and political anthropology characteristic of it and it alone.

We can call this principle of the TMW the "plurality of the prince."

Decision in the TMW

A similar fractal approach is a basic attitude of the TMW in relation to all other classic IR themes, connected with sovereignty, the legitimacy of actors, the legality of procedures in international relations, etc. In all cases, the correct answer will be appeal to the unique social and cultural character of each civilization, without any *a priori* projection. The TMW demands of the theoretician maximum *civilizational apperception*, i.e. the ability to reflect on his own belonging to the civilization from whose position he is carrying out the analysis of international relations, and penetration into the civilizational value system of the studied civilization. Fully relevant here is the demand made on cultural anthropologists who plan to study some archaic society. For this, the following are necessary:

- knowledge of the language

- embedded observation

- a moratorium on hasty conclusions and moral comparisons of the "stranger" with "oneself"

- the absence of preconceived opinions and prejudices about the studied culture

- the sincere intention to delve into how the members of a given society themselves understand and interpret their surrounding world, social institutions, traditions, symbols, rituals, etc.

Boas and his students systematized and justified this perfectly.

The TMW demands of the political scientist or international relations scholar skills of social and cultural anthropology, without which no conclusion regarding the political structures of some or another civilization and the correlations among these structures will have validity or scientific worth.

Hence, questions relating to the problem of sovereignty, its bearers, and its structure demand preliminarily a deep comprehension of the civilizational field. As a convenient formula for the precise fixation of where concretely the strategic pole is located in a civilization, we can use the procedure proposed by Schmitt for determining sovereignty. "Sovereign is he who decides in an exceptional situation," he asserted. An exceptional situation is a situation when the legal code, responsible for ordering questions of rule under normal circumstances, ceases to be in effect and cannot serve as a basis for choosing one or another course of action, involving significant groups of people and having broad social consequences. This definition by Schmitt is a convenient instrument for localizing the center of authority in problematic historical circumstances. If we use this criterion, then any decision made in an exceptional situation automatically means the *localization* of the pole of sovereignty. He who decides in exceptional circumstances is sovereign, even when he does not have enough legality or legitimacy from a legal perspective. And, on the contrary, he who does not decide in exceptional circumstances is not sovereign, even if he has formal legality and legitimacy.

We thus get a concrete parameter for determining the location of the sovereign instance in practically *any legal system* — both where authority operates openly and transparently (*potestas directa*) and where it acts indirectly and secretly (*potestas indirecta*). So, in a civilization, given its natural indeterminacy and the complexity of the social layers within a general context, the position of the sovereign, the prince, is determined *through* the actual localization of the source of decisions made, and not vice-versa. *He who decides in exceptional circumstances is the prince, the bearer of sovereignty.*

This observation about decision allows us to treat a civilization as a system open to history and saturated with powerful existential energy. At some moment, any civilization in a multipolar world has to make a decision. And each time the channel of this decision can theoretically arise *in a different segment of the civilization.* This complicates extremely the structure of international law and makes it partly spontaneous and "occasionalistic" (ad hoc). But at the same time, it frees the natural element of historical being, full of inner power, *potestas*, from the necessity of constantly transgressing the system of legal norms, which becomes a limitation and constrains the current of vital, unpredictable history.

Here, the concept of the "chaos of international relations," present in classical paradigms, too, is entirely appropriate and relevant. The sphere of international relations in the context of the TMW is "chaos" to the extent that it allows decision to manifest at any point of a civilization, whether predictable or not. The challenging of decision and restraint of its elements, the formalization and legitimization of authority, all of this is an internal affair of each civilization. But theoretically we should examine *sovereignty not as a legal postulate, but as a function of the very fact of the decision made in exceptional circumstances.* In this case, the strategic poles of civilizations will constantly be dealing with a series of spontaneous challenges, and the drama of history will acquire a rich, organic, dynamic character — in contrast to the routine, military or pacifistic, into which international relations have transformed in the Westphalian era or under bipolarity, the doleful apogee of which is the weak-willed utopia of globalization. The point of decision-making in exceptional circumstances is the concretization of the historic spirit; not the dispersion of anatomical wishes and the simplest instincts, but movement along the vertical of intensive historical process.

Elites and Masses in the TMW

Practically the same thing can be said about the social stratification of civilizations and the distinction in them of higher and lower classes, "elites and masses," according to Pareto. The geometry of the social heights and social depths can vary in each civilization. The holism of non-Western civilizations can be caste, estate, theocratic, ethnic, monarchical, democratic, mixed — anything. Theoretically, Western society can also become anything, although on the basis of empirical observation we can suppose that it will preserve into the future its individualistic and liberal-democratic attitudes and tendencies and the dispersion of the social body toward atomization and civil society. And that is the West's full right — to organize its society in accordance with its own will. Democratization and dispersion of authoritative powers, however, do not change the principal class inequality and the huge gap between the super-rich elite and all other citizens. So class inequality, which was industriously concealed in the 20th century by the growth of the middle class, which lately has slowed dramatically, constitutes for its part the elites and masses of the West in the sense of the hierarchies described in detail and criticized by Marxists. Elites and masses in the West are formed through class criteria. The West considers this "normal" and "just," and other forms of hierarchization are rejected as "inhumane," "barbarous," and "non-democratic."

The West is fully justified in making any political decisions with respect to its own society. But in regard to non-Western societies in a multipolar world, the West loses its competence as a moral judge. People of the European culture of the modern era think that material inequality is "just," and social inequality is not. Members of other civilizations, Hindu, for instance, have an entirely different opinion. The logic of *dharma* and the laws of *artha* lead the Hindu to a completely different kind of justice: it is just to follow traditions, including the caste tradition, and unjust to transgress them. The noble pauper who fulfills his karma is reincarnated in the higher world. The negligent rich man has every chance to be reincarnated as a pig. And this is just. But the invasion of Western criteria into the structure of traditional society is the height of injustice and a typically colonial and racist practice in its roots.

It is unjust for Muslims for a bank to take a percentage (since time belongs to Allah, and money cannot beget money in time, this is blasphemy and sacrilege, infringement of the prerogative of the Lord of Worlds). At the same time, the stratification of Islamic society can seem unacceptable to Hindus, while Chinese Confucianists might see in Buddhism "covert anarchy" and "asociality."

Each civilization has elites and masses, upper and lower strata. And they have their functions in the social body in accordance with the normative configurations of this body. In some cases, they can influence foreign policy and act as "competent groups" (in contrast to the certainty among classical realists that the lambda-individual, the member of the masses, has null-competence in international questions); in other cases, they cannot, and then their share of influence in international relations is insignificant.

But this question again depends on the case of the specific civilization under examination. Neither neoliberal concepts about the steadfast and guaranteed growth of the competence of the masses in international relations, nor realist skepticism on this account are applicable as a norm in the TMW.

The social stratification of societies in a civilization is not an international problem, does not have a universal form, and is dealt with through the strategic center of civilization, however it might be constituted: as government, parliament, emperor, ruling party, the union of spiritual leaders, etc. The social body itself, the civilizational *holos*, makes this center legitimate.

Dialogue and the War of Civilizations

Now, let us outline how the TMW considers the problem of war in IR. War is a feature of human history, an event constantly encountered in it. Moreover, according to generally accepted conceptions, precisely war and revolution make history history. Practically all known states were created by wars or emerged in the course of military campaigns. Wars laid the basis for practically all historically existing elite groups.

War, according to Heraclitus, "is the father of all things; in some, it reveals gods; in others, people; in some, slaves, in others, free men." The *polis* as a state and politics as governance of the *polis* were always closely connected with the elements of war, internally, in regard to the main task of ensuring security, and from the perspective of military campaigns against an external enemy.

To strive for an end of wars is the same as to strive for the abolishment of history or the disappearance of the human and human society. To minimalize the risk of war or get rid of it altogether can be the task of certain cultures or social or gender types (women are not inclined to the element of war and regard it most often as a catastrophe and purely negative phenomenon). But observation of the history of human societies shows that peace and war are cyclically alternating phenomena, replacing one another in a certain succession, however long or short the intervals might be.

Consequently, the TMW does not preclude the possibility of war (conflict) between civilizations, but neither does it think that this is the sole possible scenario.

Here we should turn to the concept of *dialogue*. Dialogue is in Greek "conversation with someone else," where utterances are transmitted (*dia* — from one to another). Dialogue can be expressed in words, but also in gestures. But words and gestures can be peaceful or aggressive, depending on the situation. Dialogue can be harsh. In the final analysis, *war can also be a form of dialogue*, during which one side *communicates* something to the other side in a harsh manner.

Dialogue does not necessarily imply the equality of the speakers. The very structure of human language is hierarchical, so the pronunciation of phrases in a dialogue can full well bear the character of a deployment of the will to power or strategy of domination. This confirms again that war can also be regarded as a dialogue.

In the TMW, there implicitly unfolds between civilizations precisely dialogue, which can be considered in two extremes: peaceful dialogue and non-peaceful dialogue. But in any case at issue is precisely communication, the intercourse of one with another, and, accordingly, the socialization of a civilization or several civilizations at once in the general system of international relations. Civilizations are constantly in dialogue with each other. Sometimes the dialogues last millennia, during which peoples, cultures, and religions mix, intersect, come closer to one another, absorb one another, separate and move away from one another, etc. Hence, it is not possible to *begin* a dialogue between civilizations and it is not possible to *end* it. It goes on by itself, and all human history can be regarded as an *uninterruptedly continuing dialogue.*

But civilizations become the main actors of international relations only under certain circumstances. According to the TMW, today we are living in precisely such a situation, and so the structure of the dialogue of civilizations demands a new comprehension and heightened reflection. Precisely today, this dialogue needs *formalization.* How, about what, and to what end do civilizations dialogue with each other?

The dialogue of civilizations is the constitution of the basic pair of identities "we" and "they," which is an integral part of any society. Society can recognize itself as itself only before a different society *apprehended* as an other. Since a civilization is a maximally complex system of society, consisting, in the first place, of both hierarchical and juxtaposed layers and strata, the degree of this civilizational reflectiveness about its own identity requires special instruments, much more complex than the models and procedures of identification for other basic units. Civilizational identity, both for self-assertion and for opposing itself to another, and, accordingly, for forming the figure of the other, demands the highest extent of complex reflection. As a rule, this level is expressed in a particular philosophy or theology, a spiritual tradition, concentrated in the intellectual elite, but tangentially touching all social strata, right to its very depths. That which is the philosophy or theology for the elites becomes the typical look of the mentality, psychology, and average cultural type for the masses. But on every level, from the keen awareness of philosophical foundations to the most inertial and unconscious mental and psychological clichés, through historical events, political reforms, progress in the arts and sciences and in economic practices — the identity of a civilization is asserted, and in being asserted as such necessarily contrasts with the identity of other, neighbouring civilizations. This is the dialogue of civilizations: the constant comparison of one's own and the foreign, the discovery of common characteristics or, by contrast, differences, the exchange of separate elements and rejection of others, the disclosure of meanings or semantic shifts that distort the elements of another civilization. In certain cases, the presence of the other becomes the basis for wars. In others, dialogue develops peacefully and constructively.

Civilizations dialogue with one another about the constantly redefined balance of mine and thine, identity and otherness. This dialogue has no final goal, since it does not set before itself the task of convincing the other of one's rightfulness or, the more so, in adopting the figure of the other as normative for oneself (also in some cases of extreme expansion or extreme passivity, this, too, can happen). But the purpose is not the attainment of a goal, but rather the dialogue itself, which in the open historical process always shrouds itself in a sequence of historical events arising in various spheres: from religious and political reforms and the appearance of new philosophical theories to popular uprisings, dynastic overthrows, military campaigns, cycles of economic growth and decline, new discoveries, expansions and contractions, ethnic migrations, etc. The whole multilevel structure of civilization participates in the dialogue, and it is carried on throughout all its stages. However, the dialogue is formalized by the intellectual elite, who are able capaciously to reflect and determine the parameters of their own identity and the identity of the other. To a significant extent, they configure the figure of the other, ascribe to it these or those traits, correctly or incorrectly surmise the semantic blocs of the civilization with whom they are in dialogue.

In increasing the level of a civilization's formalization, the role of the intellectual elite also grows substantially, since it becomes the bearer of the dialogue of civilizations not merely by inertia, but according to its own function. And this function acquires a highly important international dimension, since the very structure of international relations in a multipolar world depends directly on the structure of the dialogue of civilizations. If the strategic pole is the place of making *decisions* and the point of the civilization's sovereignty, the substantial, *semantic* center of a civilization is concentrated in its intellectual elite, which under multipolarity sharply increases its status in the domain of international life. This elite is empowered to saturate multipolarity with semantic content and to unfold substantial processes constitutive for the sphere of international relations, and, consequently, for the history of humanity.

In the dialogue of civilizations, the intellectual elite should execute a discount [*diskont*] of all the major factors: economic, technological, material, resource, logistical, etc. Sign, image, concept, philosophical theory, and theological exegesis represent the main synthetic message from one civilization to another. And the curve of world history — war or peace, conflict or cooperation, collapse or ascension, will largely depend on what this message will be in each case.

The dialogue at issue cannot be reduced to competition, to the establishment of hegemonic relations, to convincing others of one's rightfulness, etc. The dialogue of civilizations is an irreducible, fractal field of free and spontaneous history, not programmed, and unpredictable, since the future in this case is considered a constituted horizon of thought and will. Thought concerns the area of competence of the civilization's intellectual elite; will, the strategic pole and the point of decision. Together, these two principles comprise the *hologram of the civilization*, its living, symbolic mediastinum, the solar plexus of the civilizational nervous system.

Neither authority, nor economy, nor material resources, nor competition, nor security, nor interests, nor comfort, nor survival, nor pride, nor aggression is the basic motivation of the historical being of civilizations in a multipolar world, but precisely the process of spiritual dialogue, which can on any bend or under any circumstances acquire a positive and peaceful or aggressive and martial character. "Spiritual battles," as Rimbaud wrote in *A Season in Hell*, "are as brutal as the battles of men." It is obvious that contemporary Western civilization is tired of history and no longer inspired by the high horizons of its freedom. Hence, the aspiration to be done with it as quickly as possible, to close the historical process. But the specific character of the TMW consists precisely in opening and winning back the possibility of looking at the world, at time and the era, not only with the eyes of the West; but this means that the dialogue of civilizations is conceived of not as something mechanical, routine, and having the sole goal of "no more war," but as something saturated, alive, unpredictable, tense, substantial, risky, and with an open and unknown finale.

Diplomacy: Anthropology and Traditionalism

Classical theories of IR distinguish a special group of authorized persons occupied with planning and conducting the foreign policy of the state: the diplomatic community. Its significance in international relations is great, since the entire structure of international relations depends to a significant extent on the competence and effectiveness of diplomats. Diplomats do not determine foreign policy. This decision is located as a rule on the level of the head of state or another executive organ. But the diplomatic community transforms the decision into reality, and quite a lot in international relations often depends on how artfully the diplomat does this. So, in the Westphalian system, the occupation of diplomat requires special preparation, familiarity with diverse standards and national psychology, certain skills in the conduct and manner of negotiation. Most often, diplomats are the social elite and are recruited from the highest strata.

Multipolarity makes some additional demands of the diplomatic community. Intercivilizational relations amount to dialogue. And in times of peace this dialogue acquires its highest formulation in the acts of precisely the diplomatic community that represents one civilization to another. Thus, diplomacy in the context of the TMW acquires a qualitatively new dimension: it is entrusted with the mission of the skillful conduct of intercivilizational dialogue. We saw earlier that in the TMW, the civilization's intellectual elite is responsible for this dialogue. Accordingly, the diplomatic community should be an integral part of this elite. Belonging to the intellectual elite implies a deep extent of reflection concerning the identity of one's civilization, including its multidimensional and diverse layers and non-linearities. So a member of the intellectual elite should by definition be distinguished by his remarkable skills in the domain of philosophy (and/ or theology). This demand is fully made of diplomats, too. But at the same time, another important competence is required of diplomats who act in the name of a civilization: the ability to understand the structure of *the other civilization*, with which the given one is in dialogue, and hence to master or create anew a correct system of translation (even approximately) of meaning of one civilization in the context of another. Besides reflecting on his own identity, the diplomat of a multipolar world should be able to embrace *another identity*, to penetrate into it to a depth critically important for mutual understanding. This requires possession of a certain *topos* that could be approximately common to the most diverse civilizational contexts.

In this connection, we should immediately reject Western hegemonism, which claims universal explanation of the main attitudes about society, politics, and the world (on the basis of the criteria and norms of Western civilization itself). The Western versions of the humanitarian disciplines (philosophy, history, sociology, law, political science, cultural studies, etc.) are shot through with ethnocentrism and striving for epistemological hegemony. So reliance on this basis takes us out of the context of multipolarity, and in the apparent convenience of appealing to the systematization of culture and philosophy worked out by the West, this simple path proves to be the longest and leads nowhere, i.e. is unacceptable. It should be rejected as obviously unfit for the formation of a diplomatic community in a multipolar world.

Only on the periphery of Western science and philosophy can we find certain methods and theories that might provide important conceptual support for the education of the professional participants of the dialogue of civilizations. In the first place, we find *cultural and social anthropology*, whose members elaborated a method of study of archaic societies, setting before themselves the goal of ridding themselves of the projection of West-centric theories onto the social object of study. Anthropologists developed a system of rules that allows them to get as close as possible to the lifeworld of non-Western societies, to clarify the structure of those societies' symbolic and mythological ideas, and to sort out complex taxonomies that do not lie on the surface (and often contrast sharply with the systematizations customary to someone from the West). At the same time, within the context of Western science the anthropological methods are applied almost exclusively to illiterate cultures, leaving the analysis of more complex societies (civilizations) to the classical disciplines: philosophy, history, sociology, religious studies, etc. In the context of a multipolar world, the anthropological approach can be successfully applied to the study of civilizations. And if we strictly follow the rules of cultural anthropology, there is a chance to obtain specialists and intellectuals who really do not depend on the epistemological hegemony of the West, and who are at the same time able to reach the deep civilization codes differing from their own and to deconstruct the identities and complexes of identity characteristic of them.

Diplomacy in the TMW should be firmly attached to anthropology, and diplomatic competences should be based on the skillful possession of the basic habits of anthropological praxis.

A second way of systematizing intercivilizational diplomacy in a multipolar world is *traditionalist philosophy*. The majority of civilizations existing today are varieties of traditional societies with a relatively low extent of modernization. In traditional society, religion, the sacred, symbol, ritual, and myth play, as is well known, a decisive role. Different religions are based on their own original theological complexes, which are either irreducible to others or are reducible, but with a huge amount of detail covering the initial meaning. Efforts to build syncretic models to facilitate interconfessional dialogue will not come to anything, since they will quickly come up against opposition of the conservative orthodoxy and will only provoke a wave of protest in the civilizations themselves. So neither a secular (Western) basis nor religious syncretism can serve as the foundation for diplomatic practice in the domain of interconfessional relations, to which important aspects of the dialogue of civilizations will come to a significant extent.

In this situation, there is only one solution: to take as the foundation the philosophy of traditionalism (Guénon, Evola, Eliade, etc.), which represents the project of clarifying the the semantic map common to traditional society as such, especially in its opposition to the secular, Western society of the modern era. But this secular society of the West, too, is analyzed by traditionalists *from the perspective of traditional society*, which makes this an optimal method for the majority of civilizations.

A full-fledged and semantically correct dialogue between civilizations can be built only on the basis of traditionalist philosophy.

After distinguishing the main directions of multipolar diplomacy, we get a theoretical basis for its establishment. Other requirements—familiarity with the technological conditions of another civilization, with military, technical, and strategic aspects, demography, ecology, social and material problems, etc., are naturally part of the necessary training for professional diplomats. But the dialogue of civilizations requires first of all *the establishment of a channel for the correct transmission of meanings.* Without this channel, the entire complex of technical knowledge will be deprived of its solid base and will become useless and perverted knowledge. Not questions of war and peace, trade or blockade, migration or security should stand at the head of multipolar diplomacy, but rather questions of the meaning of philosophy, the circulation of ideas (in the Platonic sense). Thus, diplomacy should be transformed into a kind of sacred profession.

Economy in the TMW

By the rules of contemporary discourse, no theory and no project can do without an economic program and the calculations and computations corresponding to it. The question naturally arises: on what economic model will the multipolar world be based?

In the case of a unipolar or global world, we are dealing with a single answer: the contemporary model of economics is a capitalist system, and in the future all projects will be built on this basis. At the same time, it is practically an axiom that capitalism has entered its *third phase* of development (postindustrial economy, information society, economy of knowledge, turbocapitalism, according to Luttwak, etc.), characterized by:

- the significant dominance of the financial sector over the industrial and agricultural sectors;
- disproportionate growth of the specific weight of the stock market, hedge funds, and other purely financial institutions;
- high market volatility;

- the development of transnational networks;

- the absorption by the third sector (service sector) of the second (manufacturing) and first (agricultural);

- delocalization of industry from the countries of the "rich North" to the countries of the "poor South";

- global division of labor and growth in influence of transnational corporations;

- sharp increase in high technology (high-precision and information technology);

- increase in the significance of virtual space for the development of economic and financial processes (electronic exchanges, etc.).

This is a picture of the global economy in the present and if things will continue by inertia, the near future. However, *such an economic model is not compatible with multipolarity*, since at its basis lies the implementation of Western codes of conduct of the economy on a global scale, the homogenization of the economic practices of all societies, the abolition of civilizational differences, and hence the reduction of all civilizations into a cosmopolitan system acting in accordance with universal rules and protocols first formed and applied by the capitalist West in its own interests. The contemporary global economy *is a hegemonic phenomenon*. Neo-Marxists in IR describe this compellingly, but it is also admitted by realists and liberals. Postpositivist theories (critical theory and postmodernism) are largely directed against this hegemony. The preservation of this economic system is incompatible with the realization of the multipolar project. So the TMW must have recourse to alternative economic theories.

It is useful in this regard to closely examine the Marxist and neo-Marxist critique of the capitalist system and their analysis of its fundamental contradictions, as well as the clarification and prediction of the nature of inevitable crises. Marxists often speak of the systematic

failure of capitalism and see its manifestations in the waves of the economic crises that shook humanity starting in 2008 after the collapse of
the American mortgage system. Although Marxists themselves think
that the financial crisis of capitalism will happen only after the final
internationalization of the world-system and the two global classes
(the global bourgeoisie and the global proletariat), their interpretation
of crises and prediction of their intensification is entirely realistic. In
contrast to Marxists, supporters of the TMW should not put multipolarity aside until the period that follows globalization. It is entirely
possible that the near-term crises will bring a fatal blow against the
capitalist system, without waiting for the completion of globalization
and the cosmopolitization of classes. This can well lead to a full-scale
Third World War. But in any case, the global economic model that
exists today will in the nearest future most likely suffer a fundamental
and irreversible crisis. And it will probably stop existing, at least in
its present form. The most recent borders of expansion of the new
economy and post-industrial order are apparent today, and it is not
difficult to notice that in a few steps the system will collapse.

What can the TMW oppose to post-industrialism in the economic
sphere? Our points of reference should be:

- the overthrow of the capitalist hegemony of the West;

- rejection of the pretensions of the liberal economy and market
  model to universalism and globally self-evident normativity and,
  consequently,

- economic pluralism.

The multipolar economy should be based on the principle of different
poles in the economic map of the world, too. The prospects of economic alternatives should be sought in the field of philosophy, which
rejects or at least relativizes the significance of the material, hedonis-
tic factor. Acknowledgement of the material world as the sole, most
important thing, and material success as the highest social, cultural,

and spiritual value inevitably leads us to capitalism and liberalism, i.e. to agreement with the rightfulness of the economic hegemony of the West. Even if non-Western countries will want to turn economic processes to their favor and underline the West's monopoly on control in the domain of the market economy globally, sooner or later the logic of capital will impose on non-Western countries and civilizations all the norms that exist today. Marxists are right about this: capital has its own logic, and once it is accepted, it leads the social and political system to a bourgeois form, identical to the Western one. So to act against the hegemony of the "rich North" and to express loyalty to the capitalist system is a total contradiction and a fundamental conceptual barrier on the path to the establishment of true multipolarity.

The American sociologist Sorokin clearly saw the limits of the materialistic Western civilization. From his perspective, an economy-centric society based on hedonism, individualism, consumerism, and comfort, is doomed to quick disappearance. It will be replaced by an ideational society, which has as its cornerstone radically spiritual and sometimes anti-material values. This prognosis can be a guiding thread for the TMW in its relation to economics generally. If we see in multipolarity precisely tomorrow's day, and not a mere continuation of today, we must follow the intuition of this outstanding sociologist.

Today, the majority of Western and non-Western economists are convinced that there is no alternative to the market economy. Such confidence is equivalent to confidence that all societies are moved by inclination toward material comfort and consumerism, and, consequently, that there can be no multipolarity. If we admit that economics is fate, we automatically admit that the liberal economy is fate, and in this case the economic hegemony of the "rich North" becomes natural, justified, and legitimate. It only remains for other countries to "develop quickly," which will bring the world-system to globalization, class stratification, and the abolition of the borders of civilizations (here, Wallerstein is entirely correct).

From here the logical conclusion follows that the economic model of the multipolar world should be built on the rejection of economy-centrism and on setting economic factors below social, cultural, religious, and political factors. *Not material, but the idea is fate*, and, consequently, economics should not dictate what to do in the political sphere, but the political sphere should dominate over economic motivations and structures. Without the relativization of economics, without subordinating the material to the spiritual, without transforming the economic sphere into a subordinate and secondary dimension of civilization as such, multipolarity is unattainable.

Consequently, the TMW should reject all types of economy-centric conceptions, both liberal and Marxist (since in Marxism the economy is also thought of as historical fate). Anti-capitalism, and especially anti-liberalism, should become the guiding vectors of the establishment of a TMW.

We can take as positive reference points the spectrum of alternative concepts that until today remain marginal among classical economic theories (for entirely understandable hegemonic reasons).

As a first step in the destruction of the global economic system as it is today, we should probably turn to List's theory of "the autarky of large spaces," which proposes the creation of closed economic zones on territories belonging to a shared civilization.[1] The theory suggests erecting trade barriers along the perimeter of these territories, which are formed to stimulate, within the limits of the civilization, production of the necessary minimum of goods and services required for the satisfaction of the population's needs and the development of the domestic production potential. External trade between "large spaces" is preserved, but is organized so that no one "large space" becomes dependent on foreign supplies. This guarantees the restructuring of the entire economic system in each civilization in accordance with regional particularities and the needs of the internal market. Since

---

1   Dugin, A. "The End of Economics."

civilization is by definition a demographically weighty area, having an internal market will be enough for intensive development.

At the same time, we should immediately raise the question of the creation of systems of regional currencies and rejection of the dollar as the global reserve currency. Each civilization should issue its own independent currency, secured by the economic potential of a given "large space." The polycentrism of currencies will thus become a direct expression of economic multipolarity. We should also reject any kind of universal standard in intercivilizational settlements; the course of currencies should be determined by the qualitative structure of the external trade among two or more civilizations.

The cornerstone should be the *real economy*, corresponding to the volume of concrete goods and services.

Acceptance of these rules will create the preconditions for further diversification of the economic models of each civilization. Leaving the space of global liberal capitalism and organizing "large spaces" in accordance with civilizational peculiarities (still on a market level), civilizations will further be able to elaborate their economic models themselves, according to cultural and historical traditions. In Islamic civilization, there will probably be a moratorium on bank interest. In other civilizations, there might be a turn toward socialistic practices of redistribution through some model or other (through management of the tax system, according to the theory of the French economist Sismondi, or through other instruments, right up to the introduction of a planned economy and dirigist methods).[2]

The economic pluralism of civilizations should be established gradually, without any universal instructions. Different societies will be able to create different economic models, whether market, mixed, or planned, on the basis of either the economic practices of traditional society or new post-industrial technologies. The most important thing is to demolish liberal dogmatism and the hegemony of capitalistic

---

2   Ibid.

orthodoxy, and to undermine the global function of the "rich North" as the main beneficiary in the organization of the planetary division of labor. The division of labor should develop only within "large spaces," or else a civilization will prove dependent on another, which risks engendering new hegemonies.

Media in the TMW

Mass media plays a huge role in the contemporary structure of international relations. It creates a single planetary informational environment, which more and more influences international processes. Media becomes global, and through media discourse facilitates the processes of globalizaton (in the interests of the West). The global mass media is an extremely important instrument for the West in forming social opinion and is essentially an instrument of *global rule*. To built a multipolar world, it is necessary to start a frontal attack against the globalistic mass media.

The role of the mass media in a traditional society is very limited. Its growth of influence is directly connected with modernity, bourgeois democracy, and civil society. The mass media is a constitutive element of democracy and claims to embody an *additional dimension*, between the authorities and society, elites and masses. In the space of mediacracy, a new model normative type is formed, which influences the masses *as a veiled injunction* instituting the special ontology of democratic society (what the media mentions exists; what it does not mention does not exist). For the authorities, mass media substitutes for social opinion; i.e., it is a *surrogate of the masses*. Thus, the space of mass media should in theory remove the tension between the heights and depths of society, translating their hierarchical relations into the *horizontal flatness of the television screen* (the newspaper, the computer, the pad, the mobile telephone, etc.). Mediaspace is a *double simulacrum*: a simulacrum of authority and a simulacrum of society.[3] Globalization spreads this principle to all humanity, transforming it into a global simulacrum. In mass media we encounter the projected reality of global government and the idea of an analogously projected (from below) reality of planetary society. This gives rise to a certain virtual world, which embodies in itself a global hegemonic construct projected by capital and the West. The independence of the mass media from nation-states makes it a privileged area for dissipative postmodern structures. Hence, in this domain the transition from modernity to postmodernity is most apparent, and virtuality replaces reality most perceptibly.

The global mass media creates models in non-Western countries for the national mass media, arranging them under the general virtual project. And as the role of mass media grows, the structures of traditional society prove either to be in a blind spot or are subject to planned and systematic attacks, meant to weaken and smear them.

In its nature, mass media is bourgeois and bears the mark of Western culture. So for the construction of a TMW, it is necessary to seriously reconsider its role in society. We can identify two stages on this path. The first stage consists of creating a network of *civilizational mass media*, which would serve as the constant mouthpiece of integrational processes and would facilitate the consolidation of civilizational identity. In this case, the civilizational mass media could undermine the monopoly of the global (and hence subject to the interests of the West) mass media and create the preconditions for the consolidation of cultural and social groups around the axis of a common civilization.

The second phase will consist in returning mass media into the context of the structure of the society that will be built on a civilizational basis, taking into account the particular cultural code. We cannot exclude the possibility that in some civilizations the phenomenon of mass media will be abolished, since no universal norms concerning

---

3   Dugin, A. *Pop-Culture and the Signs of the Times*. St. Petersburg: Amphora, 2005.

this question will remain, and the decision about how to organize relations between the authorities and society, elites and masses, will be decided on the basis of free civilizational quest. Some civilizations might keep this space of "democratic simulacra" and the virtual doubling of reality, while others might well prefer to refuse it.

Summary

The following table summarizes the content that the main themes of concepts of IR receive in the TMW (see below).

Our theoretical propositions constitute a prolegomenon to a full-fledged TMW. The task in this chapter was to clarify the content of the concept of "multipolarity," to relate the TMW to the existing theories of IR, and to begin to formulate some of the basic principles of this theory. Our analysis can be looked at as preparing the ground for the full construction of a developed TMW. We have on the whole marked out the main paths of this development. But a detailed elaboration of these directions is a matter for the future and still awaits execution.

The pluralism contained in the very foundation of the multipolar approach excludes any form of dogmatism. It is useless to argue about the details of the multipolar order, the rate of establishing this order, the localization of borders between civilizations, and the nuances of the legal formulation of the new system of international relations. Even the precise number of actors in the multipolar world remains an open question for now.

It was fundamental to make a theoretical break, away from the utterly vague and indefinite use of the term "multipolarity," "multipolar world," toward the theoretical basis, in light of which it acquires a fully concrete, though open for further consideration, content.

Themes	Subthemes	TMW
Actors	Quantity	Several Poles
	Subjects	Civilizations
	Political Institutionalization	*Politeia*
	Structure	Plural
Geopolitics	Main Geopolitical Concept	Large Spaces
	Borders	Poles/Zones Frontiers
Environment	Global Institution	None
International Relations	Structure	Anarchy among Civilizations
	Hegemony	Regional Hegemony Commonwealth
The Prince	Authority	Our Prince / *Princeps Nostrum* Hierarchy (content depends on civilization) Sovereignty of *Politeia*
	Decision	Competence of the Prince on the basis of Tradition
War	Possibility	Open
	Peace	Intracivilizational *Pax Nostrum*
	Security	Civilizational Security
Interests	Interests	Civilizational Interests
	Values	Civilizational Values

Themes	Subthemes	TMW
	Power	Spiritual/Material Qualitatively Plural (Depends on the Civilization)
International Political Economy	Paradigm	Plural Paradigms / Autarky of Large Spaces
	Division of Labor	Intracivilizational
Mass Media	Structure	Civilizational
	Significance	Secondary

Appendix

Theory Talk #66: Alexander Dugin

Sunday, December 7, 2014

(Source: http://www.theory-talks.org/2014/12/theory-talk-66.html)

Alexander Dugin on Eurasianism, the Geopolitics of Land and Sea, and a Russian Theory of Multipolarity

R HAS LONG been regarded as an Anglo-American social science. Recently, the discipline has started to look beyond America and England, to China (*Theory Talk* #51, *Theory Talk* #45), India (*Theory Talk* #63, *Theory Talk* #42), Africa (*Theory Talk* #57, *Theory Talk* #10) and elsewhere for non-Western perspectives on international affairs and IR theory. However, IR theorists have paid little attention to Russian perspectives on the discipline and practice of international relations. We offer an exciting peek into Russian geopolitical theory through an interview with the controversial Russian geopolitical thinker Alexander Dugin, founder of the International Eurasian Movement and allegedly an important influence on Putin's foreign policy. In this *Talk*, Dugin—among others—discusses his Theory of a Multipolar World, offers a staunch critique of western and liberal IR, and lays out Russia's unique contribution to the landscape of IR theory.

What, according to you, is the central challenge or principal debate within IR and what would be your position within this debate or towards that challenge?

The field of IR is extremely interesting and multidimensional. In general, the discipline is much more promising than many think. I think that there is a stereometry today in IR, in which we can distinguish a few axes right away.

The first, most traditional axis is realism—the English school—liberalism.

If the debates here are exhausted on an academic level, then on the level of politicians, the media, and journalists, all the arguments and methods appear new and unprecedented each time. Today, liberalism in IR dominates mass consciousness, and realist arguments, already partially forgotten on the level of mass discourse, could seem rather novel. On the other hand, the nuanced English school, researched thoroughly in academic circles, might look like a "revelation" to the general public. But for this to happen, a broad illumination of the symmetry between liberals and realists is needed for the English school to acquire significance and disclose its full potential. This is impossible under the radical domination of liberalism in IR. For that reason, I predict a new wave of realists and neorealists in this sphere, who, being pretty much forgotten and almost marginalized, can full well make themselves and their agenda known. This would, it seems to me, produce a vitalizing effect and diversify the palette of mass and social debates, which are today becoming monotone and auto-referential.

The second axis are bourgeois versions of IR (realism, the English school, and liberalism all together) vs. Marxism in IR. In popular and even academic discourse, this theme is entirely discarded, although the popularity of Wallerstein (*Theory Talk* #13) and other versions of world-systems theory shows a degree of interest in this critical version of classical, positivist IR theories.

The third axis is postpositivism in all its varieties vs. positivism in all its varieties (including Marxism). IR scholars might have got the

impression that postmodern attacks came to an end, having been successfully repelled by 'critical realism', but in my opinion it is not at all
so. From moderate constructivism and normativism to extreme post-
structuralism, postpositivist theories carry a colossal deconstructive
and correspondingly scientific potential, which has not yet even
begun to be understood. It seemed to some that postmodernism is a
cheerful game. It isn't. It is a new post-ontology, and it fundamentally
affects the entire epistemological structure of IR. In my opinion, this
axis remains very important and fundamental.

The fourth axis is the challenge of the sociology of international
relations, which we can call 'Hobson's challenge'. In my opinion, in his
critique of eurocentrism in IR, John M. Hobson laid the foundation
for an entirely new approach to the whole problematic by proposing
to consider the structural significance of the "eurocentric" factor as
dominant and clarifying its racist element. Once we make eurocentrism a variable and move away from the universalist racism of the
West, on which all systems of IR are built, including the majority
of postpositivist systems (after all, postmodernity is an exclusively
Western phenomenon!), we get, theoretically for now, an entirely different discipline—and not just one, it seems. If we take into account
differences among cultures, there can be as many systems of IR as
there are cultures. I consider this axis extremely important.

The fifth axis, outlined in less detail than the previous one, is
the Theory of a Multipolar World vs. everything else. The Theory of
a Multipolar World was developed in Russia, a country that no one
ever took seriously during the entire establishment of IR as a discipline—hence the fully explainable skepticism toward the Theory of a
Multipolar World.

The sixth axis is IR vs. geopolitics. Geopolitics is usually regarded
as secondary in the context of IR. But gradually, the epistemological
potential of geopolitics is becoming more and more obvious, despite
or perhaps partially because of the criticism against it. We have only
to ask ourselves about the structure of any geopolitical concept to

discover the huge potential contained in its methodology, which takes us to the very complex and semantically saturated theme of the philosophy and ontology of space.

If we now superimpose these axes onto one another, we get an extremely complex and highly interesting theoretical field. At the same time, only one axis, the first one, is considered normative among the public, and that with the almost total and uni-dimensional dominance of IR liberalism. All the wealth, 'scientific democracy', and gnoseological pluralism of the other axes are inaccessible to the broad public, robbing and partly deceiving it. I call this domination of liberalism among the public the 'third totalitarianism', but that is a separate issue.

How did you arrive at where you currently are in your thinking about IR?

I began with Eurasianism, from which I came to geopolitics (the Eurasianist Petr Savitskii quoted the British geopolitician Halford Mackinder) and remained for a long time in that framework, developing the theme of the dualism of Land and Sea and applying it to the actual situation. That is how the Eurasian school of geopolitics arose, which became not simply the dominant, but the only school in contemporary Russia. As a professor at Moscow State University, for six years I was head of the department of the Sociology of International Relations, which forced me to become professionally familiar with the classical theories of IR, the main authors, approaches, and schools. Because I have long been interested in postmodernism in philosophy (I wrote the book *Post-Philosophy* on the subject), I paid special attention to postpositivism in IR. That is how I came to IR critical theory, neo-Gramscianism, and the sociology of IR (John Hobson, Steve Hobden, etc.). I came to the Theory of a Multipolar World, which I eventually developed myself, precisely through superimposing geopolitical dualism, Carl Schmitt's theory of the *Großraum*, and John Hobson's critique of Western racism and the eurocentrism of IR.

In your opinion, what would a student need in order to become a specialist in IR?

In our interdisciplinary time, I think that what is most important is familiarity with philosophy and sociology, led by a paradigmatic method: the analysis of the types of societies, cultures, and structures of thought along the line Pre-Modernity — Modernity — Post-Modernity. If one learns to trace semantic shifts in these three epistemological and ontological domains, it will help one to become familiar with any popular theories of IR today. Barry Buzan's theory of international systems is an example of such a generalizing and very useful schematization. Today an IR specialist must certainly be familiar with deconstruction and use it at least in its elementary form. Otherwise, there is a great danger of overlooking what is most important.

Another very important competence is history and political science. Political science provides generalizing, simplifying material, and history puts schemas in their context. I would only put competence in the domain of economics and political economy in third place, although today no problem in IR can be considered without reference to the economic significance of processes and interactions. Finally, I would earnestly recommend to students of IR to become familiar, as a priority, with geopolitics and its methods. These methods are much simpler than theories of IR, but their significance is much deeper. At first, geopolitical simplifications produce an instantaneous effect: complex and entangled processes of world politics are rendered transparent and comprehensible in the blink of an eye. But to sort out how this effect is achieved, a long and serious study of geopolitics is required, exceeding by far the superficiality that limits critical geopolitics (Ó Tuathail et. al.): they stand at the beginning of the decipherment of geopolitics and its full-fledged deconstruction, but they regard themselves as its champions. They do so prematurely.

What does it entail to think of global power relations through a spatial lens (*Myslit prostranstvom*)?

This is the most important thing. The entire philosophical theme of Modernity is built on the dominance of time. Kant already puts time on the side of the subject (and space on the side of the body, continuing the ideas of Descartes and even Plato), while Husserl and Heidegger identify the subject with time altogether. Modernity thinks with time, with becoming. But since the past and future are rejected as ontological entities, thought of time is transformed into thought of the instant, of that which is here and now. This is the basis for the ephemeral understanding of being. To think spatially means to locate Being outside the present, to arrange it in space, to give space an ontological status. Whatever was impressed in space is preserved in it. Whatever will ripen in space is already contained in it. This is the basis for the political geography of Friedrich Ratzel and subsequent geopoliticians. Wagner's *Parsifal* ends with the words of Gurnemanz: 'Now time has become space'. This is a proclamation of the triumph of geopolitics. To think spatially means to think in an entirely different way [*topika*]. I think that postmodernity has already partly arrived at this perspective, but has stopped at the threshold, whereas to cross the line it is necessary to break radically with the entire axiomatic of Modernity, to really step over Modernity, and not to imitate this passage while remaining in Modernity and its tempolatry. Russian people are spaces [*Russkie lyudi prostranstva*], which is why we have so much of it. The secret of Russian identity is concealed in space. To think spatially means to think 'Russian-ly', in Russian.

Geopolitics is argued to be very popular in Russia nowadays. Is geopolitics a new thing, from the post-Cold War period, or not? And if not, how does current geopolitical thinking differ from earlier Soviet (or even pre-Soviet) geopolitics?

It is an entirely new form of political thought. I introduced geopolitics to Russia at the end of the 80s, and since then it has become extremely popular. I tried to find some traces of geopolitics in Russian history, but besides Vandam, Semyonov-Tyan-Shansky, and a few short articles by Savitskii, there was nothing. In the USSR, any allusion to geopolitics was punished in the harshest way (see the 'affair of the geopoliticians' of the economic geographer Vladimir Eduardovich Den and his group). At the start of the 90s, my efforts and the efforts of my follow-ers and associates in geopolitics (=Eurasianism) filled the worldview vacuum that formed after the end of Soviet ideology. At first, this was adopted without reserve by the military (The Military Academy of the General Staff of the Armed Forces of Russia), especially under Igor Rodionov. Then, geopolitics began to penetrate into all social strata. Today, this discipline is taught in the majority of Russian universi-ties. So, there was no Soviet or pre-Soviet geopolitics. There is only the contemporary Eurasian school, which took shape at the end of the 80s. *Foundations of Geopolitics* was the first programmatic text of this school, although I had published most of the texts in that book ear-lier, and some of them were circulated as texts in government circles. Recently, in 2012, I released two new textbooks: *Geopolitics* and *The Geopolitics of Russia*, which together with *The War of Continents* are the results of work in this field, along four axes.

In your book *International Relations*, not yet published in English, you set out your Theory of a Multipolar World as a distinct IR the-ory. What are the basic components of the Theory of a Multipolar World—and how is it different from classical realism?

In order to be understood and not get into the details, I can say that the Theory of a Multipolar World seriously and axiomatically adopts Samuel Huntington's thesis about the plurality of civilizations. Russia has its own author, who claimed the same thing more than a hundred years ago: Nikolay Danilevsky, and then the Eurasianists. However, everything starts from precisely this point: civilization is not one, but many. Western civilization's pretension to universalism is a form of the will to domination and an authoritarian discourse. It can be taken into account but not believed. It is nothing other than a strategy of suppression and hegemony. The following point follows: we must move from thinking in terms of one civilization (the racism of eurocentric versions of IR) to a pluralism of subjects. However, unlike realists, who take as the subject of their theory nation-states, which are themselves products of the European, bourgeois, modern understanding of the Political, the Theory of a Multipolar World proposes to take civilizations as subjects. Not states, but civilizations. I call them 'large *politeiai*', or civilizations, corresponding to Carl Schmitt's 'large spaces'. As soon as we take these civilizations—'large politeiai'—as subjects, we can then apply to them the full system of premises of realism: anarchy in the international system, sovereignty, the rationality of egoistic behavior, etc. But within these *politeiai*, by contrast, a principle more resembling liberalism, with its pacifism and integration, operates, only with the difference that here we are not talking about a 'planetary' or 'global' world, but about an intra-civilizational one; not about global integration, but about regional integration, strictly within the context of civilizational borders. Postpositivism, in turn, helps here for the deconstruction of the authoritarian discourse of the West, which masks its private interests by 'universal values', and also for the reconstruction of civilizational identity, including with the help of technological means: civilizational elites, civilizational media, civilizational economic algorithms and corporations, etc. That is the general picture.

Your theory of multipolarity is directed against the intellectual, political, and social hegemony of the West. At the same time, while drawing on the tools of neo-Marxist analysis and critical theory, it does not oppose Western hegemony 'from the left', as those approaches do, but on the basis of traditionalism (René Guénon, Julius Evola), cultural anthropology, and Heideggerian phenomenology,

or 'from the right'. Do you think that such an approach can appeal to Anglo-American IR practitioners, or is it designed to appeal mainly to non-Western theorists and practitioners? In short, what can IR theorists in the West learn from the theory of multipolarity?

According to Hobson's entirely correct analysis, the West is based on a fundamental sort of racism. There is no difference between Lewis Morgan's evolutionary racism (with his model of savagery, barbarism, civilization) and Hitler's biological racism. Today the same racism is asserted without a link to race, but on the basis of the technological modes and degrees of modernization and progress of societies (as always, the criterion "like in the West" is the general measure). Western man is a complete racist down to his bones, generalizing his ethnocentrism to megalomaniacal proportions. Something tells me that he is impossible to change. Even radical critiques of Western hegemony are themselves deeply infected by the racist virus of universalism, as Edward Said showed with the example of 'orientalism', proving that the anticolonial struggle is a form of that very colonialism and eurocentrism. So the Theory of a Multipolar World will hardly find adherents in the Western world, unless perhaps among those scholars who are seriously able to carry out a deconstruction of Western identity, and such deconstruction assumes the rejection of both Right (nationalist) and Left (universalist and progressivist) clichés. The racism of the West always acquires diverse forms. Today its main form is liberalism, and anti-liberal theories (most on the Left) are plagued by the same universalism, while Right anti-liberalisms have been discredited. That is why I appeal not to the first political theory (liberalism), nor the second (communism, socialism), nor to the third (Fascism, Nazism), but to something I call the Fourth Political Theory (or 4PT), based on a radical deconstruction of the subject of Modernity and the application of Martin Heidegger's existential analytic method.

Traditionalists are brought in for the profound critique of Western Modernity, for establishing the plurality of civilizations, and for rehabilitating non-Western (pre-modern) cultures. In Russia and Asian countries, the Theory of a Multipolar World is grasped easily and naturally; in the West, it encounters a fully understandable and fully expected hostility, an unwillingness to study it carefully, and coarse slander. But there are always exceptions.

What is the Fourth Political Theory (4PT) and how is it related to the Theory of a Multipolar World and to your criticism of the prevailing theoretical approaches in the field of IR?

I spoke a little about this in the response to the previous question. The Fourth Political Theory is important for getting away from the strict dominance of Modernity in the sphere of the Political, for the relativization of the West and its re-regionalization. The West measures the entire history of Modernity in terms of the struggle of three political ideologies for supremacy (liberalism, socialism, and nationalism). But since the West does not even for a moment call into question the fact that it thinks for all humanity, it evaluates other cultures and civilizations in the same way, without considering that in the best case the parallels to these three ideologies are pure simulacra, while most often there simply are no parallels. If liberalism won the competition of the three ideologies in the West at the end of the 20th century, that does not yet mean that this ideology is really universal on a world scale. It isn't at all. This episode of the Western political history of modernity may be the fate of the West, but not the fate of the world. So other principles of the political are needed, beyond liberalism, which claims global domination (=the third totalitarianism), and its failed alternatives (Communism and Fascism), which are historically just as Western and modern as liberalism. This explains the necessity of introducing a Fourth Political Theory as a political frame for the correct basis of a Theory of a Multipolar World. The Fourth Political Theory is the direct and necessary correlate of the Theory of a Multipolar World in the domain of political theory.

Is IR an American social science? Is Russian IR as an academic field a reproduction of IR as an American academic field? If not, how is IR in Russia specifically Russian?

IR is a Western scientific discipline, and as such it has a prescriptive, normative vector. It not only studies the West's dominance, it also produces, secures, defends, and propagandizes it. IR is undoubtedly an imperious authoritarian discourse of Western civilization, in relation to itself and all other areas of the planet. Today the US is the core of the West, so naturally in the 20th century IR became more and more American as the US moved toward that status (it began as an English science). It is the same with geopolitics, which migrated from London to Washington and New York together with the function of a global naval empire. As with all other sciences, IR is a form of imperious violence, embodying the will to power in the will to knowledge (as Michel Foucault explained). IR in Russia remains purely Western, with one detail: in the USSR, IR as such was not studied. Marxism in IR did not correspond to Soviet reality, where after Stalin a practical form of realism (not grounded theoretically and never acknowledged) played a big role—only external observers, like the classical realist E.H. Carr, understood the realist essence of Stalinism in IR. So IR was altogether blocked. The first textbooks started to appear only in the 90s and in the fashion of the day they were all liberal. That is how it has remained until now. The peculiarity of IR in Russia today lies in the fact that there is no longer anything Russian there; liberalism dominates entirely, a correct account of realism is lacking, and postpositivism is almost entirely disregarded. The result is a truncated, aggressively liberal and extremely antiquated version of IR as a discipline. I try to fight that. I recently released an IR textbook with balanced (I hope) proportions, but it is too early to judge the result.

Stephen Walt argued in a September article in *Foreign Policy* that Russia 'is nowhere near as threatening as the old Soviet Union', in

part because Russia 'no longer boasts an ideology that can rally supporters worldwide'. Do you agree with Walt's assessment?

There is something to that. Today, Russia thinks of itself as a nation-state. Putin is a realist; nothing more. Walt is right about that. But the Theory of a Multipolar World and the Fourth Political Theory, as well as Eurasianism, are outlines of a much broader and large-scale ideology, directed against Western hegemony and challenging liberalism, globalization, and American strategic dominance. Of course, Russia as a nation-state is no competition for the West. But as the bridgehead of the Theory of a Multipolar World and the Fourth Political Theory, it changes its significance. Russian policies in the post-Soviet space and Russia's courage in forming non-Western alliances are indicators. For now, Putin is testing this conceptual potential very gingerly. But the toughening of relations with the West and most likely the internal crises of globalization will at some point force a more careful and serious turn toward the creation of global alternative alliances. Nevertheless, we already observe such unions: The Shanghai Cooperation Organization, BRICS, the Eurasian Union—and they require a new ideology. Not one like Marxism, any universalism is excluded, but also not simple realist maneuvers of regional hegemons. Liberalism is a global challenge. The response to it should also be global. Does Putin understand this? Honestly, I don't know. Sometimes it seems he does, and sometimes it seems he doesn't.

Vladimir Putin recently characterized the contemporary world order as follows: 'We have entered a period of differing interpretations and deliberate silences in world politics. International law has been forced to retreat over and over by the onslaught of legal nihilism. Objectivity and justice have been sacrificed on the altar of political expediency. Arbitrary interpretations and biased assessments have replaced legal norms. At the same time, total control of the global mass media has made it possible when desired to portray white as

black and black as white'. Do you agree with this assessment? If so, what is required as a response to this international situation?

These are true, but rather naïve words. Putin is just indignant that the West establishes rules in its own interests, changes them when necessary, and interprets allegedly 'universal norms' in its own favor. But the issue is that this is the structure of the will to power and the very organization of logo-phallo-phono-centric discourse. Objectivity and justice are not possible so long as speech is a monologue. The West does not know and does not recognize the other. But this means that everything will continue until this other wins back the right to recognition. And that is a long road. The point of the Theory of a Multipolar World is that there are no rules established by some one player. Rules must be established by centers of real power. The state today is too small for that; hence the conclusion that civilizations should be these centers. Let there be an Atlantic objectivity and Western justice. A Eurasian objectivity and Russian justice will counter them. And the Chinese world or *Pax Sinica* [world/peace: same word in Russian] will look different than the Islamic one. Black and white are not objective evaluations. They depend on the structure of the world order: what is black and what is white is determined by one who has enough power to determine it.

How does your approach help us understand Russia's actions on the world stage better than other IR approaches do? What are IR analyses of Russia missing that do not operate with the conceptual apparatus of multipolarity?

Interesting question. Russia's behavior internationally is determined today by the following factors:

First, historical inertia, accumulating the power of precedents (the Theory of a Multipolar World thinks that the past exists as a structure; consequently, this factor is taken into account from many sides and in detail, while the 'tempocentrism' [Steve Hobden, John Hobson] of classical IR theories drops this from sight. We have to pay attention to this, especially taking into consideration the fact that Russia is in many ways still a traditional society and belongs to the 'imperial system' of IR.) There are, besides, Soviet inertia and stable motives ('Stalinism in IR');

Second, the projective logic of opposition to the West, stemming from the most practical, pragmatic, and realist motivations (in the spirit of Caesarism, analyzed by neo-Gramscians) will necessarily lead Russia (even despite the will of its leaders) to a systemic confrontation with American hegemony and globalization, and then the Theory of a Multipolar World will really be needed (classical IR models, paying no attention to the Theory of a Multipolar World, drop from sight the possible future; i.e., they rob themselves of predictive potential because of purely ideological prejudices and self-imposed fears).

But if an opponent underestimates you, you have more chances to land an unexpected blow. So I am not too disturbed by the underestimation of the Theory of a Multipolar World among IR theorists.

In the Western world, the divide between academia and policy is often either lamented ('ivory tower') or, in light of the ideal of academic independence, deemed absent. This concerns a broader debate regarding the relations between power, knowledge and geopolitics. How are academic-policy relations in Russia with regards to IR and is this the ideal picture according to you?

I think that in our case both positions have been taken to their extreme. On one hand, today's authorities in Russia do not pay the slightest attention to scholars, dispatching them to an airless and sterile space. On the other hand, Soviet habits became the basis for servility and conformism, preserved in a situation when the authorities for the first time demand nothing from intellectuals, except for one thing: that they not meddle in sociopolitical processes. So the situation with science is both comical and sorrowful. Conformist scholars follow the authorities, but the authorities don't need this, since they do not so much go anywhere in particular as react to facts that carry themselves out.

If your IR theory isn't based on politically and philosophically liberal principles, and if it criticizes those principles not from the Left but from the Right, using the language of large spaces or *Großraum*, is it a Fascist theory of international relations? Are scholars who characterize your thought as 'neo-Fascism', like Andreas Umland and Anton Shekhovstov, partially correct? If not, why is that characterization misleading?

Accusations of Fascism are simply a figure of speech in the coarse political propaganda peculiar to contemporary liberalism as the third totalitarianism. Karl Popper laid the basis for this in his book *The Open Society and Its Enemies*, where he reduced the critique of liberalism from the Right to Fascism, Hitler, and Auschwitz, and the criticism of liberalism from the Left to Stalin and the GULAG. The reality is somewhat more complex, but George Soros, who finances Umland and Shekhovstov and is an ardent follower of Popper, is content with reduced versions of politics. If I were a Fascist, I would say so. But I am a representative of Eurasianism and the author of the Fourth Political Theory. At the same time, I am a consistent and radical anti-racist and opponent of the nation-state project (i.e. an anti-nationalist). Eurasianism has no relation to Fascism. And the Fourth Political Theory emphasizes that while it is anti-liberal, it is simultaneously anti-Communist and anti-Fascist. I think it isn't possible to be clearer, but the propaganda army of the 'third totalitarianism' disagrees and no arguments will convince it. 1984 should be sought today not where many think: not in the USSR, not in the Third Reich, but in the Soros Fund and the 'Brave New World'. Incidentally, Huxley proved to be more correct than Orwell. I cannot forbid others from calling me a Fascist, although I am not one, though ultimately this reflects badly not so much on me as on the accusers themselves: fighting an imaginary threat, the accuser misses a real one. The more

stupid, mendacious, and straightforward a liberal is, the simpler it is
to fight with him.

**Does technological change in warfare and in civil government chal-
lenge the geopolitical premises of classical divisions between spaces
(Mackinder's view or Spykman's heartland-rimland-offshore continents)? And, more broadly perhaps, does history have a linear or
a cyclical pattern, according to you?**

Technological development does not at all abolish the principles of
classical geopolitics, simply because Land and Sea are not substances,
but concepts. Land is a centripetal model of order, with a clearly
expressed and constant axis. Sea is a field, without a hard center, of
processuality, atomism, and the possibility of numerous bifurcations.
In a certain sense, air (and hence also aviation) is aeronautics. And
even the word astronaut contains in itself the root *nautos*, from the
Greek word for ship. Water, air, outer space—these are all versions of
increasingly diffused Sea. Land in this situation remains unchanged.
Sea strategy is diversified; land strategy remains on the whole constant. It is possible that this is the reason for the victory of Land over
Sea in the last decade; after all, capitalism and technical progress are
typical attributes of Sea. But taking into consideration the fundamental character of the balance between Leviathan and Behemoth,
the proportions can switch at any moment; the soaring Titan can be
thrown down into the abyss, like Atlantis, while the reason for the
victory of thalassocracy becomes the source of its downfall. Land
remains unchanged as the geographic axis of history. There is Land
and Sea even on the internet and in the virtual world: they are axes
and algorithms of thematization, association and separation, group-
ings of resources and protocols. The Chinese internet is terrestrial; the
Western one, nautical.

You have translated a great number of foreign philosophical and geopolitical works into Russian. How important is knowledge transaction for the formation of your ideas?

I recently completed the first release of my book *Noomachy*, which is entirely devoted precisely to the Logoi of various civilizations, and hence to the circulation of ideas. I am convinced that each civilization has its own particular Logos. To grasp it and to find parallels, analogies, and dissonances in one's own Logos is utterly fascinating and interesting. That is why I am sincerely interested in the most varied cultures, from North American to Australian, Arabic to Latin American, Polynesian to Scandinavian. All the Logoi are different and it is not possible to establish a hierarchy among them. So it remains for us only to become familiar with them. Henry Corbin, the French philosopher and Protestant, who studied Iranian Shiism his entire life, said of himself 'We are Shiites'. He wasn't a Shiite in the religious sense, but without feeling himself a Shiite, he would not be able to penetrate into the depths of the Iranian Logos. That is how I felt, working on *Noomachy* or translating philosophical texts or poetry from other languages: in particular, while learning Pierce and James, Emerson and Thoreau, Poe and Pound, I experienced myself as 'we are Americans'. And in the volume devoted to China and Japan, as 'we are Buddhists'. That is the greatest wealth of the Logos of various cultures: both those like ours and those entirely unlike ours. And these Logoi are at war; hence *Noomachy*, the war of the intellect. It is not linear and not primitive. It is a great war. It creates that which we call the 'human', the entire depth and complexity, which we most often underestimate.

Final question. You call yourself the 'last philosopher of empire'. What is Eurasianism and how does it relate to the global pivot of power distributions?

Eurasianism is a developed worldview, to which I dedicated a few books and a countless number of articles and interviews. In principle, it lies at the basis of the Theory of a Multipolar World and the Fourth Political Theory, combined with geopolitics, and it resonates with Traditionalism. Eurasianism's main thought is plural anthropology, the rejection of universalism. The meaning of empire for me is that there exists not one empire but at minimum two, and even more. In the same way, civilization is never singular; there is always some other civilization that determines its borders. Schmitt called this the Pluriverse and considered it the main characteristic of the Political. The Eurasian Empire is the political and strategic unification of Turan, a geographic axis of history in opposition to the civilization of the Sea or the Atlanticist Empire. Today, the USA is this Atlanticist Empire. Kenneth Waltz, in the context of neorealism in IR, conceptualized the balance of two poles. The analysis is very accurate, although he erred about the stability of a bipolar world and the duration of the USSR. But on the whole he is right: there is a global balance of empires in the world, not nation-states, the majority of which cannot claim sovereignty, which remains nominal (Stephen Krasner's 'global hypocrisy'). For precisely that reason, I am a philosopher of empire, as is almost every American intellectual, whether he knows it or not. The difference is only that he thinks of himself as a philosopher of the only empire, while I think of myself as the philosopher of one of the empires, the Eurasian one. I am more humble and more democratic. That is the whole difference.

OTHER BOOKS PUBLISHED BY ARKTOS

OTHER BOOKS PUBLISHED BY ARKTOS

OTHER BOOKS PUBLISHED BY ARKTOS

OTHER BOOKS PUBLISHED BY ARKTOS

ERNST VON SALOMON	*It Cannot Be Stormed*
	The Outlaws
PIERO SAN GIORGIO	*CBRN: Surviving Chemical, Biological, Radiological & Nuclear Events*
	Giuseppe
SRI SRI RAVI SHANKAR	*Celebrating Silence*
	Know Your Child
	Management Mantras
	Patanjali Yoga Sutras
	Secrets of Relationships
GEORGE T. SHAW (ED.)	*A Fair Hearing*
FENEK SOLÈRE	*Kraal*
WERNER SOMBART	*Traders and Heroes*
OSWALD SPENGLER	*Man and Technics*
RICHARD STOREY	*The Uniqueness of Western Law*
TOMISLAV SUNIC	*Against Democracy and Equality*
	Homo Americanus
	Postmortem Report
	Titans are in Town
ASKR SVARTE	*Gods in the Abyss*
HANS-JÜRGEN SYBERBERG	*On the Fortunes and Misfortunes of Art in Post-War Germany*
ABIR TAHA	*Defining Terrorism*
	The Epic of Arya (2nd ed.)
	Nietzsche's Coming God, or the Redemption of the Divine
	Verses of Light
JEAN THIRIART	*Europe: An Empire of 400 Million*
BAL GANGADHAR TILAK	*The Arctic Home in the Vedas*
DOMINIQUE VENNER	*For a Positive Critique*
	The Shock of History
HANS VOGEL	*How Europe Became American*
MARKUS WILLINGER	*A Europe of Nations*
	Generation Identity
ALEXANDER WOLFHEZE	*Alba Rosa*
	Rupes Nigra

Lightning Source UK Ltd.
Milton Keynes UK
UKHW012201130223
416920UK00005B/911